Activities for Very Young Learners

Cambridge Handbooks for Language Teachers

This series, now with over 50 titles, offers practical ideas, techniques and activities for the teaching of English and other languages, providing inspiration for both teachers and trainers.

Recent titles in this series:

Activities for Very Young Learners

Herbert Puchta and Karen Elliott

Consultant and editor: Scott Thornbury

CAMBRIDGE
UNIVERSITY PRESS

CAMBRIDGE
UNIVERSITY PRESS

University Printing House, Cambridge CB2 8BS, United Kingdom

One Liberty Plaza, 20th Floor, New York, NY 10006, USA

477 Williamstown Road, Port Melbourne, VIC 3207, Australia

4843/24, 2nd Floor, Ansari Road, Daryaganj, Delhi – 110002, India

79 Anson Road, #06–04/06, Singapore 079906

Cambridge University Press is part of the University of Cambridge.

It furthers the University's mission by disseminating knowledge in the pursuit of education, learning and research at the highest international levels of excellence.

www.cambridge.org
Information on this title: www.cambridge.org/9781316622735

© Cambridge University Press 2017

First published 2017
20 19 18 17 16 15 14 13 12 11 10 9 8 7 6 5 4 3 2 1

Printed in Spain by GraphyCems

A catalogue record for this publication is available from the British Library

ISBN 978-1-316-62273-5 Paperback
ISBN 978-1-316-62283-4 Apple ibook
ISBN 978-1-316-62278-0 Google ebook
ISBN 978-1-316-62274-2 Kindle ebook
ISBN 978-1-316-62284-1 ebooks.com ebook

Additional resources for this publication at http://esource.cambridge.org/activitiesforvyl

Contents

Thanks

Herbert's dedication

To Niklas Puchta with love.

Karen's dedication

To Aitxiber García Fernández and all teachers starting on their journey of teaching English to very young children.

We would like to thank Scott Thornbury, our series editor, for his constructive comments and his valuable suggestions on the various drafts of the manuscript. We thoroughly enjoyed working with you, Scott!

We would like to thank most warmly the team at Cambridge University Press: Karen Momber, Publisher, for inviting us to write this book, for the encouragement and guidance throughout the writing process, and especially the comments on the first draft of the introduction. Jo Timerick, Senior Editor, for her enthusiasm and support, especially during the production of the book, and her help in putting together the online resources. Lucy Frino, Freelance Editor, for helping us decide what not to include in the book after it turned out that the original manuscript was far too long for the series, for her love of detail and her painstaking work on the manuscript.

Herbert would like to thank Günter Gerngross for many insightful discussions over the years on how young learners learn, and on the importance of stories in that process. Many thanks go to Caroline Petherick on her comments on parts of the first draft of the manuscript.

Karen has had the privilege of working with many teachers of very young children over the years. A special mention for invaluable support in the area of classroom management goes to Itxaso Valdajos, Liz Beer and Caoimhe Hurley. Thank you so much Edith Hatton and Rowan Hardman for your creativity and enthusiasm for art in the classroom. I have much gratitude to Ana Esther de Diego and Elixabete Redondo for the times we have spent working on projects together. For being as enthusiastic about phonics as I am, thank you Mary Ockenden, Aitziber Gutierrez, Marisa Solares and Sarah Richards. For her insights into teaching very young learners I would like to thank Maria Suarez. With fond memories of three-year old Sarah Rouben, who showed me how we learn to read, and finally thank you Tim Bacon, for your unwavering support and for collaborating on the songs and chants which appear on the website.

Finally, a big round of applause goes to the children in various classes that we have had the pleasure to work with, for their enthusiasm and energy, and for being the constant source of inspiration and fun without which this book would not have been written.

Acknowledgements

The authors and publishers acknowledge the following sources of copyright material and are grateful for the permissions granted. While every effort has been made, it has not always been possible to identify the sources of all the material used, or to trace all copyright holders. If any omissions are brought to our notice, we will be happy to include the appropriate acknowledgements on reprinting and in the next update to the digital edition, as applicable.

Text

Günter Gerngross for the text on p. 80. Copyright © Günter Gerngross. Reproduced with kind permission.

Photo

Key: B = Below, R = Right, C = Centre, L = Left, T = Top

p. 118, p. 123, p. 124, p. 125 (T), p.125 (B), p. 126, p. 127, p. 128, p. 129, p. 130, p. 131, p. 132, p. 133, p. 142, p. 144, p. 146, p.147, p. 156, p. 169, p. 170: Courtesy of Karen Elliott; p. 90: Nidwlw/ iStock/Getty Images Plus/Getty Images; p. 153 (Key): Malerapaso/E+/Getty Images; p. 153 (Duck): Floortje/E+/Getty Images; p. 153 (Stick): Ivanastar/E+/Getty Images; p. 153 (Pencil): Denis Winkler/ EyeEm/Getty Images; p. 153 (Coin): Pando Hall/Photographer's Choice/Getty Images; p. 153 (Stone): Michele Constantini/PhotoAlto Agency/Getty Images; p. 153 (Ball): JoKMedia/Getty Images; p. 153 (Eraser): Andy Roberts/The Image Bank/Getty Images; p. 168 (T): Auki/Getty Images/Getty Images; p. 168 (B): Jobalou/DigitalVision Vectors/Getty Images/Getty Images; p. 185 (T): Topform84/ iStock/ Getty Images Plus/Getty Images; p. 185 (B): Vip2807/iStock/Getty Images Plus/Getty Images.

Illustrations by Peter Allen p. 82

The publishers are grateful to the following contributors: Ian Harker at Soundhouse Studios: online chant and song recordings (1.2 *We are stars*, 3.1 *The classroom chant*, 3.3 *The shapes pointing song*, 3.6 *I can jump, I can hop*, 3.8 *Have some chicken*); Karen Elliott: all other online chant and song recordings; Isabel Escalante: commissioned illustrations.

Introduction

About this book

Why did we write this book?

There is a growing trend – almost global – towards lowering the starting age for children learning English as a second or foreign language. It is now not uncommon for three and four year-olds to attend English classes, and although such tuition is more often found in private institutions, state kindergartens may also provide English classes to children from the age of five or younger.

As writers, teacher trainers and teachers involved in teaching English to the very young, we felt inspired to write a book dedicated to this intriguing age group. The educational needs of these learners are different from those of older children, and our aim is to encourage teachers to reflect on these needs and understand more fully the role they play when educating the whole child. We feel that providing quality language tuition is about creating naturally meaningful experiences that encourage very young children to view themselves positively and become enthusiastic about learning the new language.

Who is it for?

This book is for teachers and teaching assistants working with three- to seven year-olds who are learning English as a foreign or second language. It is for teachers in kindergarten or the first year of primary school, for those teaching in extra-curricular programmes in institutes or academies and for those teaching privately. The book is also for those studying to become teachers of very young learners who are looking for ideas and activities to engage their future pupils in meaningful and imaginative ways.

If you are an experienced teacher of very young children who is looking for new ideas and activities, you may want to skip this Introduction. If you know what kind of activity you are looking for, check the Contents page for the relevant category, and find the activities which seem suitable for your class. By browsing through the information at the beginning of each activity you should be able to decide if it is appropriate, before continuing to read the instructions in more detail.

Alternatively, you might prefer to start by scanning through each chapter, making notes of the activities you wish to use with your class. With most of the activities, you will find suggestions for variations or extensions. Of course, you may then come up with your own ideas on how to change, extend or adapt an activity to the specific needs of your group of learners.

If you are a novice teacher or a teacher trainee, or have previously taught English to older learners, you might like to develop your understanding of very young learners and find out about some of the important principles behind teaching this age group.

In this Introduction, we aim to provide information on the learning characteristics of this age group, how to create an optimal learning atmosphere in the classroom, and the qualities of classroom interaction that support children's learning processes in a natural way. You will find an outline of our educational vision, including the reasons why we believe that learning a foreign language early in life – with the proper help – can make a significant contribution to the overall development of young children.

Our views on teaching very young learners are based not only on some crucial research findings, but on our own classroom experiences, classroom observations and discussions with colleagues from a variety of countries. We encourage teachers to become conscious of their own educational vision through understanding child language development and child development in general.

How is this book structured?

The book starts with a series of practical tips and suggestions for the very young learner's classroom called *Tips for teaching very young learners*. The tips are organized into topics such as lesson planning, classroom management and observation techniques. They include practical ideas on how best to handle the challenges that typically arise in the young learners' classroom.

The main part of the book consists of a wide range of practical activities for use in the classroom. The majority do not require much preparation, and where drawings or handouts are needed, you can usually find them as illustrations or on separate photocopiable pages. The handouts and other materials can also be downloaded from the dedicated website. Material which is available to download is marked with the symbol [↖].

The activities are organized into eight chapters:

1 Class routines and classroom management
2 Movement and games
3 Songs, chants and rhymes for topics
4 Stories and storytelling
5 Arts, crafts and displays
6 Exploring the world
7 Thinking-based activities
8 Pronunciation and early literacy.

About very young learners

What is a very young learner?

Our term 'very young learners' refers to children between the ages of three and seven, who are just setting out on their educational journey. They are still making the transition towards being part of a group and understanding the meaning and structure of their educational life. They may or may not attend school daily and many of them have not learned to read in their own language yet.

Human beings start learning from the moment they are born and are naturally inclined to pursue activities which help them make sense of their world and their place in it. Play is central to this process, in that a child's desire to be doing things and choice of tasks is directly linked to how and what they need to learn. Learning at this age includes developing fine motor skills (for example, picking things up, colouring and cutting) and gross motor skills (for example, running, throwing and catching). For children in their early years, the huge task of understanding the natural and social world can be overwhelming, without adult guidance. We can enhance their play / learning to help them develop their confidence, co-ordination, understanding of logical sequences and thought processes by setting developmentally appropriate tasks.

How do very young children start using language?

The psychologist Jean Piaget stresses the idea that very young children are active learners. They interact with the world around them, and learning occurs because they want to solve problems posed by the environment. This is how a child's thinking is formed, and this is how a need to use language develops. The theories of the developmental psychologist Lev Vygotsky go further: they stress the important role of social interaction and language in the child's development. When a child says 'apple', for example, this one word represents a whole sentence. It is through the interaction with an adult or older sibling – through the child listening to a fluent speaker's response to their utterance 'apple' that the child is learning language. This is illustrated in an authentic example of child-caregiver language quoted in Peccei (1999, p.100):

> **Child:** (*picks up red bean bag in shape of a frog*) Santa Claus.
> **Mum:** Santa Claus? That's a frog, honey. That's not Santa Claus. That's a frog. A red frog.
> **Child:** Frog (*points to frog on car*). Sits.
> **Mum:** Yes, he's sitting down. That's right.

What we can see from the example above is how the adult almost 'speaks for the child', thus modelling important language. The mother says what the child might say if she could express herself more fully. Wood, Bruner and Ross (1976) call the support the child gets through such intervention 'scaffolding', and we will see below how the experienced language teacher can use a similar technique in the language classroom to extend what the child is able to say.

A key quality in child development is the intimate relationship between thinking and talking. Whereas older children have learned to think *before* they talk, very young children form their ideas *through* talking. For them, speech is a way to actually work out what is in their minds, and helps them to learn to understand it.

Another feature of the way very young learners start using language is that they are at an early stage of literacy development. Some may recognize a few letters – those found in their name or the first letter in some familiar words. Some may also have learned to read a few words in a holistic way – words they frequently see in their surroundings, such as the name of their favourite breakfast cereal. Although some very young children's reading skills may be more developed, they are still only just embarking on the exciting journey of making sense of the written word. This means that reading and writing are not central to the learning process in the way they will be in later years.

How do very young learners develop cognitively?

According to educational philosopher Kieran Egan (1997), a person's intellectual growth happens naturally, through certain developments deeply rooted in our cultural history. In order for a child's intellect to grow appropriately, the development of certain 'cognitive tools' is essential. It is obvious that if we want to cut a wooden board in half we need a saw – a physical tool. Likewise, if we want to solve complex problems we need 'tools of the mind'. But the fundamental difference between physical tools and tools of the mind is that the former help us to manipulate the world around us, while the latter are about controlling ourselves, our body, our thinking and our emotions. The ability to use tools of the mind is an important step on the way towards learning socially acceptable behaviour.

Below are a few of the building blocks of language that form important cognitive tools in early child development and that – as we will see later – are important teaching tools in the English language classroom too:

Rhythm and rhyme

In pre-literate days people had the ability to remember texts of sometimes epic length. Rhythm and rhyme were important mnemonic devices in this process of remembering. In our modern age it is still through rhythm and rhyme that children start remembering chunks of language. They also experience enormous joy through repeatedly hearing (and later joining in with) the rhythms and rhymes of language. Exposure to and playing with rhythm and rhyme help children develop an understanding of the patterns of language (sound patterns first) and also form cognitive tools they will later need for the understanding of structures.

Images and imaginative thinking

For young children, there is often no borderline between reality and imagination. For example, if the teacher uses a hand puppet in class, a four year-old recognizes that it is a puppet, and yet as soon as the puppet starts 'talking' (with the help of the teacher), the child reacts to it as if it were alive.

Such imaginative processes lead to the creation of images in the child's mind. Understanding oral language not only requires the knowledge of words, but also the ability to create and use mental images. There is clear evidence that learners who are at ease with creating lots of images while listening to a story, for example, remember more language from it.

Storytelling

Stories play an essential role in the cognitive development of children. The story form is something people enjoy in all cultures. However, telling stories in class, as well as entertaining children, helps them develop an understanding of the world and their own life experiences. Stories communicate information and at the same time help us to understand how we feel about it. That's why they are such a powerful form of language. Engaging very young children with stories is a time-honoured tradition which holds a central place in their language learning.

Small talk

For the very young, learning to engage in small talk is not just about getting used to an exchange of linguistic formalities. It is an important building block of cognitive development, and it has a key social function for the child. Learning to participate successfully in small talk strengthens the child's self-concept and gives him / her a feeling of security and acceptance in society. Being accepted by their teacher and classmates is an extremely important experience for the child, and at the same time it is a precondition for developing social relationships and friendships.

What is the best age for learning another language?

Folk wisdom has it that the earlier a child starts learning a new language the better, and often, from their own personal experience, parents can see the advantages of learning a language from a very young age. There is the perception that children's brains are more elastic and open, since they appear to be able to pick up languages from birth onwards.

Evidence to support this belief is often based on studies involving immigrant families. In all likelihood, it is the youngest members of an immigrant family that will succeed in adapting perfectly to the new language environment. It usually takes them just a couple of years to develop native-like competence in the new language, and they seem to assimilate with ease the culture of the target country. Meanwhile, learning the language of their adopted country seems a much more frustrating process for their grown-up relatives. The older they are, the greater their chances of failing at becoming fully-functioning members of their new speech community.

But what about children learning a new language in a more formal environment, in other words, not as immigrants to a country where the language is spoken but in their own country, in kindergartens or pre-school groups? These groups are embedded in a different language, culture and environment from the new language the children are learning. That is a different story altogether. Recent studies have challenged the idea that very young learners have a cognitive advantage when it comes to learning another language in these circumstances. These studies cast doubt on the widely-held belief that one or two lessons a week can replicate the immersion experience of immigrant children, and can lead to comparable learning outcomes. Nevertheless, if language learning is integrated into the overall curriculum and carried out as naturally as possible, it can have positive effects on children's attitudes to learning English in their subsequent education. This makes an important contribution to their lifelong learning.

Is there a critical period for language learning?

The observation that young children are at ease with learning languages, while teens and adults often struggle to achieve a good level of proficiency in a new language, led to the development of the so-called *Critical Period Hypothesis* (CPH). The hypothesis claims that the best period for learning a foreign language is between the ages of approximately 2 and 12, and that due to neurological changes, humans are unable to learn a foreign language to native-speaker standard after the onset of puberty.

Intensive research has been carried out on the CPH since it was first proposed. Although scholars agree that age has an influence on language learning, there is no agreement on whether a critical period exists, or on how age actually influences language learning.

An alternative hypothesis is that there is not just one but several critical periods for learning language. This is due to the fact that linguistic competence consists of various aspects, only some of which are difficult to acquire as we become older. According to this view, input on the syntax and phonology of language needs to be provided before a certain 'door' in a child's brain closes. However, the successful acquirement of other aspects of a language, such as lexis and rules governing word formation (known as morphology), may be less dependent on age factors. This hypothesis goes some way to explain why adults are likely to be able to learn quite complex vocabulary, while other areas of the language (such as grammar and phonology) may cause them problems.

Of course, there are examples of adult learners who do not manage to build up a solid lexicon in the target language, or who have problems with morphology. Although this can often be explained by the learners' mature age and subsequent memory loss, there may be other reasons unrelated to biology, such as limited input, insufficient motivation, and time commitments to work, family and so on.

Finally, it should be noted that despite differences in their rates of learning, both children and adults who are learning a second language make many of the same omission, substitution, and misplacement errors that occur in the acquisition of their own language. These errors are a normal part of the developmental process and occur in first language development as well as in second language development. Errors, therefore, should be viewed less as evidence of failure and more as indicators of development.

Can only children acquire perfect pronunciation in a second language?

Although there are some well-documented cases of adults who started to learn a foreign language in upper secondary school or later and managed to achieve the performance level of native speakers, this proficiency in pronunciation seems to be a fairly exceptional phenomenon amongst adult learners. A number of empirical studies confirm what teachers of young learners have frequently observed: children are usually more successful in learning the pronunciation of a new language than adults.

Should very young learners be taught reading and writing in another language?

When we teach English to very young children, we naturally concentrate on speaking and listening skills. But what about reading and writing? Although they are often considered skills better left until later in education, there are some important issues to keep in mind when deciding if you will include literacy development in your class.

We communicate and share a wealth of information through the written form of language. Our environment is filled with text: on the streets where we live and shop, on the packaging of the products we buy and the books, papers and screens we read. The reasons for reading and writing are many and varied, but at the heart of it all is communication.

Children are surrounded by text in a similar way. Even before they are reading or writing, they are involved in 'literacy events', such as sending a birthday card to a friend, helping to make a shopping list, watching the opening titles of their favourite cartoon or being read to from a picture book. And in this day and age, the text that surrounds children is often English.

It stands to reason that children are in general comfortable with seeing symbols, words and signs that they have not yet learned to decipher. There is no reason why their English classroom should not reflect the real world by also being a text-rich environment. Labels on supplies (*pencils, glue, paper*), signs (*Story corner; What's the weather like today?*) and project titles (*The life cycle of a frog; Recycling*) are a great way to indicate different areas, routine activities and current topics without putting pressure on children to actually understand the words themselves.

What we are providing is a comfortable and safe environment that includes English text. We also do this when we read to children from story books with pictures or let them look through books in a reading corner, or when we play videos of songs with words and sentences appearing on the screen. What this kind of exposure does not provide, however, is an understanding of the relationship between the English alphabetic symbols and the sounds they most often represent.

The explicit teaching of the relationship between letters and their sounds has become more common in the very young learner's classroom these days and, if done in the spirit of play, it can add significant information to children's early literacy development. It provides them with some understanding of the process of reading and gives them practice in saying and hearing the phonemes more clearly. There is some evidence that learning the sounds at the beginning and ends of words also helps children to understand the spoken language, since they can break a sentence down and hear the individual words through a process known as 'edging'. Finally, many children are very keen to read and it is a shame to hold them back when they are ready to do so.

The most important thing to keep in mind is that learning to read and write should be a pleasurable experience, full of fun and games. It should never be thrust upon the child as a test of their adequacy in the classroom. Children's first attempts at decoding words (even if they are heavily supported by accompanying images or if they are largely the result of learning something by heart), together with the first wobbly marks they make on paper, should be celebrated as a step towards a literate and independent future.

Our educational vision of teaching English to very young learners

How can we create the best learning environment for the very young?

Below you will find seven prerequisites for an optimum language learning environment:

1   **Teaching time and teaching quality.** An early language programme that aims to facilitate successful language acquisition requires intensive exposure to the language, and this requires time. But even if time is limited, the language learning experience can still be motivating for the learners; the *quality* of the learning experience can be optimized to ensure maximum engagement and interaction in the classroom.

2   **A teacher with an excellent command of the target language.** The teacher must have the ability to talk to children in a natural way, and to adapt his or her language to the children's needs. This requires great flexibility in the target language.

3   **A teacher with an innate understanding of how young children learn in natural ways.** This kind of empathy with the learner is important in any kind of educational context, but we believe it's essential for teaching early learners.

4   **A methodology that engages the learner as a whole person through multi-sensory learning processes.** This means that the children do not just watch and listen to the teacher presenting the new language, and later repeat what they have learned. They engage with the language through touch and movement *at the same time* as they are using their sight and hearing, as, for example in Total Physical Response activities (see Chapter 2). In such a classroom culture, learners will remember better what they are learning. No time is wasted on explicit grammar explanations.

5   **The right level of challenge.** In a learning culture, the level of challenge must be in proportion to the learners' prior knowledge and the skills they already have. In such an environment, learners are, at times, pushed to the limits of their present competence.

6   **Meaningful tasks,** which engage learners emotionally and can contribute to their cognitive development.

7   **A teacher who can speak the learners' own language proficiently.** If all the learners share a first language that is different from the teacher's, the teacher needs to speak their language, so that they can both anticipate comprehension problems and provide on-the-spot support, should problems occur.

How can we make the teaching of English to very young learners effective?

An effective approach to the teaching of English to very young learners will be based on a number of key building blocks or principles of teaching. The seven principles below serve as the underlying framework for the activities in the main part of this book. They are reflected in the methodology, the teaching techniques and the strategies suggested in the activities.

1 Develop thinking skills.

According to Vygotsky's approach to early childhood education, children learn how to use tools of the mind from adults. But the tools are not just handed down – they need to be facilitated, or 'scaffolded' in the shared social space between adult and child. The early language learning classroom is an ideal place for this development of thinking skills.

If, after a TPR (Total Physical Response) activity, four-year-old Olivia starts rolling around on the floor while the rest of the class is standing in a circle waiting for instructions from the teacher, Olivia doesn't yet have the right cognitive tools to help her focus on the task. So the teacher will now help her focus (through scaffolding), by pointing at other children and saying, for example, *Look at Emily. She's standing still. Look at Emma. She is standing still. And look at Freddie. He is standing still, too. And now look at yourself. You are standing still, too. Very good, Olivia. Very good. We're all standing still.*

What happens in the shared space between teacher and learner will become automatic after some time, but the teacher's role in that process is vitally important. He or she observes the child and models the behaviour required as the next step in their development. The teacher uses gestures, symbols, images, gentle touch (culture permitting), and so on, to mediate or remind the child of the desired behaviour. Children that get such support regularly will gradually learn to do independently and confidently the things they could only initially do with help from an adult.

In the example of classroom language above, the teacher facilitates a child's insight into the kind of behaviour that works best in a certain situation. In similar ways, we can help children make more of the cognitive resources they bring to the classroom. Based on the belief that 'what a child can do with help today they will be able to do independently tomorrow,' we can help children become familiar with important concepts such as number, size, shape and space, and gradually help them build a coherent model of the world. There is a whole chapter in the book (*Chapter 7: Thinking-based activities*, pages 173–194) with ideas on how to do this.

2 Provide optimal input.

Since the written representation of the new language is less accessible to very young learners, sound is extremely important and attractive to them. At this age a great deal of language learning takes place through oral and visual activities – stories, songs, chants, rhymes, images and realia – and through gestures and movements, including games with simple rules.

As mentioned earlier, there is clear evidence that children learn a new language best when they are immersed in it; that is when their parents have emigrated to a new country and the children learn the language from their environment of friends, neighbours, teachers and others using the language naturally. Schools can never totally emulate such a situation. However, we believe that it is possible in non-immersion educational contexts to create conditions that turn language learning for very young learners into a meaningful and successful activity.

Our belief is based on personal experience, and on teaching we have seen in pre-schools in many countries around the world. Admittedly, this quality of teaching, where children often have ten or more hours of English a week, is more often found in private pre-schools or kindergarten language programmes than in state educational contexts. But we have come across this quality of teaching quite frequently in private schools in countries such as Spain, Turkey, Russia, China, South Korea and various countries in Latin and Central America.

The way the teacher interacts with the children is crucial to how they learn to interact in and with the new language. In order to make the language learning experience as meaningful, enjoyable and natural as possible, teachers need to adapt the language they use to talk to their pupils in such a way that it becomes comprehensible. This requires the teacher to develop an ability that we often observe in parents, grandparents or other adult family members talking to very young children in their own language. They intuitively seem to 'get it right', so that children can understand them. It is a way of talking which is sometimes known as 'motherese' or 'caregiver talk', and it is a tactic that many of us adopt when talking to people who are less competent than we are: we use what is often called *foreigner talk*.

However, modified interaction need not always involve linguistic simplification. It may include elaboration, slower speech rate, using gesture and providing additional contextual cues such as images or realia. There are various other examples of teacher strategies which modify input, such as checking comprehension, clarification of requests and self-repetition or paraphrasing.

3   Go beyond an input–output model of learning.

Children love imitating what they see and hear, and imitation is a first important means of getting children to speak. Learning a language successfully, though, is not just about the children parroting what their teachers say. Using a language successfully is about being creative with it – and we can help learners make first steps towards this by going beyond a mere input-output model of learning.

Parents often measure the quality of their children's language learning by the amount of language they are able to produce. Small wonder then, that teachers want to get children to learn to speak the language as soon as possible, first by imitating what they hear and then by gradually learning to say things that they want to say for themselves.

Children will love imitating anything that engages them emotionally. Hence, the capacity of the input to grab their attention is vital. For example, if children love a story they hear their teacher tell, or the character voices they hear on an audio recording of a story, they are more likely to start speaking along when the teacher next revises the story with them. Likewise, a catchy tune or the rhythm of a cool chant will help children remember important chunks of language more easily, and they will love singing or saying the words themselves.

Another key point that helps young children to develop their speaking skills is that they are often chatterboxes and they love to engage in small talk. In both child and adult conversation, small talk is fairly predictable (for example, *How are you? I'm fine, thanks.*). In other words, in small talk situations, speakers often use 'formulaic' or 'prefabricated' language, rather than creating utterances by putting them together word by word. So, if the teacher regularly engages their pupils in small talk in the target language, they learn to pick up important chunks of language, and gradually learn to be 'chatty' in a very natural and useful way. And not just in the target language: some children will transfer this valuable skill to their own language, helping them become more sociable and balanced individuals.

Quality of input plays an important role in the teaching–learning process, but in order for the learning to be successful we need to look beyond an input–output model. We need to investigate the physical and social dynamics of the very young learners' classroom on the grounds that learning is not simply a cognitive process but is situated in its social context, and is physically 'embodied' through gesture, voice and movement. According to this view of language learning, we need to broaden our focus and take other factors into consideration: factors which can be defined as embodiment, embedding and extension. We need to look at how teacher and pupils are organizing their interaction using gestures, rhythm, body movements, and even teaching materials in tandem with their spoken language.

The following is an extract from a lesson in a pre-primary class of three and four year-olds that Herbert had the pleasure and the privilege to observe at the ABC private language school in Hong Kong:

The teacher is pointing at a picture in a book. It shows a smiling girl, with an apple and a piece of cake in front of her.

Teacher:	Look at the girl here. (*The teacher points at the picture.*)
	Is she happy or sad?
Children:	Happy!
Teacher:	She's so happy! Do you think she likes apples?
Children:	Yes.
Teacher:	Yes, yes, yes! (*The teacher is speaking rhythmically, using her hands to support the rhythm of the language with a circular movement.*)
	Do you think she likes cake? (*The teacher repeats the hand gestures.*)
Children:	(*Some children are mirroring the teacher's hand gestures.*) Yes, yes, yes!

In fact, there is very little language 'production' in this scene of embodied interaction. The children are basically reacting to what the teacher says by echoing her words. But it is through the way the teacher uses gestures and body movement, and through the way the pupils mirror her behaviour and echo her language that they 'co-construct' the interaction in the classroom.

The teacher prompts the learners' first reaction (*Happy!*) by pointing at the picture and asking whether the girl is happy or sad. She has introduced the word *happy* in a previous lesson but assumes that her pupils will not yet be able to recall it, so she has decided to scaffold the pupils' language by offering them a choice of two possible answers (*Is she happy or sad?*). This strategy allows her pupils to say more in the target language than they would be able to without the scaffolding.

This is what follows, and again an analysis of the interaction should focus on the multimodality of the situation, not the language alone:

Teacher:	OK, let's listen to the song first. (*While the teacher is about to start the CD, one of the children stands up and tries to go past the teacher towards the free space in front of the board.*)
	All right, Linda, can you sit down again, please?
Linda:	No!
Teacher:	(*laughing*) No?
	(Linda laughs too, and carries on moving towards the space, swaying slightly.)
Teacher:	Ah! You want to dance. (*The teacher mimes dancing.*)
	Do you want to dance?
Linda:	Yes! Dance!
Teacher:	Dance. Good girl. You want to dance.

It's fascinating to watch how the interaction unfolds. As soon as the girl notices that the teacher is about to play a song, she gets up and moves towards a free space in the classroom. This is a space the teacher has previously encouraged her pupils to use for dancing while a song was playing.

Although Linda doesn't have the language to let the teacher know that she wants to dance to the music, she firmly says 'No!'. We can sense how the interaction is embedded in the social space between teacher and pupil.

One key aspect of the interaction is the amount of rapport building that happens through the mutual mirroring of body movement and echoing of language. This assures the learner that the teacher takes her seriously in spite of her inability to fully express what she wants to say. It gives her a sense of being understood by the teacher. It assures her that her teacher is interested in what she wants to communicate, and helps her to succeed in the end.

The example above, from a very young learners' classroom, shows the complexity of successful classroom interaction. But in order for such interaction to actually happen, the teacher needs to scaffold it. The teacher must be flexible in the way he or she interacts with her pupils and have a caring and facilitating attitude towards the pupils' learning. The teacher must take their pupils seriously and be able to react to what they say (or what the teacher assumes they want to say), often through one-word sentences or simply the use of body language, as seen above.

4   Teach grammar without 'teaching' grammar.

There is no point in explaining grammar rules to very young learners. They simply do not have the cognitive capacity to handle abstract concepts, such as 'verb' or 'adjective'. Neither can they discriminate between tenses, such as 'present continuous' or 'past simple'. Grammar will evolve naturally for very young learners, just as it has done in their own language, if we create the appropriate conditions in the classroom.

Children learn grammar through hearing, imitating, noticing, remembering and trying to apply language, not through meta-grammatical explanations, as we can see from this extract from a lesson.

The class are doing a simple counting activity with fruit, and they hear the teacher say various number + noun combinations:

Teacher:	(*The teacher puts an apple on the table.*) Look what we've got here: one apple.
Children:	One apple.
Teacher:	Very good. It's one apple. And now look.
	(*The teacher adds two more apples.*)
	One, two, three.
Children:	One, two, three.
Teacher:	Very good. Three apples. Three apples.
Children:	Three apples.
Teacher:	And now? (*The teacher puts a banana on the table.*)
Child:	One …
Teacher:	Yes! Good! One banana.
Children:	One banana.

The children enjoy this simple activity. Learning to count is fun and their success builds their self-esteem. Gradually, some of them may notice intuitively the use of the plural *apples* when there is more than one item.

Of course, children learn at different paces: some children won't notice the plural form difference in the activity above when they encounter it for the first time, but they will pick up on it later, for example, in a story or a song. This is why revision and varied input are extremely important in getting children to notice language. The more they hear and grow familiar with a form of input, the more they will want to imitate the language from it and the more easily they will remember language. Then they will gradually notice the features of the material, imitate them and try to use them independently.

5   See errors as a sign of learning.

As teachers, we need to be patient, and aware of the fact that errors are signs of learning. Parents are often proud of the first few longer sentences children produce in their own language, rather than worrying about the mistakes they make. In fact, mistakes children make when they are learning to speak are frequently seen as 'cute'. As natural phenomena of child language, these errors in the first language will vanish with time and further practice.

But how should we react to errors in the language classroom? A good answer would be 'as naturally as possible'. If we understand the child's meaning despite errors, we need to respond to what they say positively and continue with the communication. We should avoid any kind of feedback that might be perceived as criticism by the child, or as an indication that something is 'wrong' about the language they have produced. The experienced teacher, perceiving an appropriate moment, will just smile and quietly repeat the correct form. This way, the child may feel like repeating it too.

But the teacher should not make corrections all the time. Nor indeed should children be expected to repeat the discreet corrections that the teacher makes. Young children have a limited attention span, and trying to get them to repeat correct versions of things they have said 'wrongly' could become a chore for both teacher and pupils. If you as a language teacher can perceive your pupils' errors as similar to the ones they make in their own language (the 'cute' mistakes), you will remember that it takes time to develop accuracy, and that you need to give your pupils that time.

Above all we need to ensure that children are not scared of making mistakes in the new language. We have to do everything we can to help them embrace this language-learning-friendly attitude toward errors as an important basis for lifelong learning.

6   Take the child's own language seriously.

It would not be wise or possible to ban the use of a pupil's own language from the young learners' classroom. It might even create stress and stop the learning process in its tracks. Learning draws on previous learning, and children's experiences with acquiring their own language are still fresh in their minds, and form a valuable platform for learning the foreign language. Not understanding anything at all in the classroom can be threatening, so the children's own language can be an important safety net.

However, the challenge for the teacher is to use as much English as possible, and resort to the children's own language in ways that facilitate the learning of the new language. Classroom experience has shown that the following strategies for using both English and the first language work well:

- *The teacher uses a 'sandwiching' technique.* They say something in English while using mime and gesture to help the children understand it, then say the same phrase or sentence in their own language (repeating the mime and gesture), and then immediately repeats the same sentence in English again (yet again repeating mime and gesture). Here is an example:

> **Teacher:**   OK, now stand up. Stand behind your chair. (*The teacher stands behind her chair.*)
> Stellt euch hinter euren Stuhl.
> Stand behind your chair.
> Good! And now close your eyes and listen. (*The teacher points at her eyes and closes them, then points at her ears.*)
> Schließt eure Augen und hört gut zu.
> Close your eyes and listen. Well done!

- *The teacher uses a puppet that can only 'speak' English*, and repeats what the puppet has said in the learners' own language, if and when necessary.
- *There are two teachers in the class.* One teacher speaks only English, while the other acts as a mediator, speaking English with their colleague and using the children's own language, if and when necessary.

There is evidence that these techniques are very efficient in getting children to understand what the teacher is saying, especially if the teacher establishes routines by regularly using certain activities and learning processes. This gives children a feeling of security, shows them that they can understand the teacher well, and makes it possible to progressively reduce the use of the children's own language.

7   See the teacher's role as educator and facilitator.

Time spent as an educator (establishing routines, helping learners to focus their attention, and so on), is not time wasted, but time well invested. This is because it helps to improve the quality of interaction in the classroom, gives the learners a sense of security and helps to make learning the focus of the classroom. Observation also facilitates learning because it helps us see our children as individuals with different needs, who are at different stages of the learning process.

One of the key challenges for teachers of very young learners is to help their learners to focus their attention. Children's eyes and ears are everywhere (frequently not where their teacher wants them to be!) and often they can barely sit still at all. They find it difficult to listen to their teacher, and especially to their classmates. When we recently asked a group of colleagues to come up with a metaphor describing how they see their own role in the young learners' classroom, one of them said, 'It's difficult to tell. I love those kids, but quite often I feel like a lion tamer, and sometimes, well, more like a clown … trying to get their attention through all kinds of tricks.'

Many children are exposed for several hours a day to screens filled with colourful, fast-moving images, accompanied by high-volume digital sound effects. Most educators view this well-known phenomenon critically, yet so-called 'teaching games' and 'educational TV programmes' for children use those very ingredients to grab children's attention successfully. Once children are used to this kind of sensory bombardment, it will be difficult for teachers to grab their attention without a similar approach. Little wonder, then, that some teachers feel that in order to reach out to their younger pupils they need to 'sing and dance like Big Bird', as one colleague put it.

If getting your students to focus their attention is an important issue for you too, you will find that this book offers lots of ideas and practical activities to draw on. Have a look at the *Tips for teaching very young learners* (pages 16–30), for example. They will help you with planning, setting up routines, marking the stages of a lesson clearly and using a wide variety of different activities (including changing the pace of a lesson according to your perception of the interest level / mood of the class). The multi-sensory activities in Chapter 6 (pages 149–172) are also a very effective way to engage learners, and the suggestions in Chapter 7 (pages 173–194) provide guidance in helping students to focus and develop their thinking skills.

Summary of some key points

- Research does not support the commonly-held belief that very young children are the best language learners whatever the circumstances, neither is there any clear evidence in favour of a critical period for language learning.
- In natural learning contexts very young children will effortlessly and rapidly acquire native-like proficiency. As language teachers, we are well advised to create classroom cultures that come close to the qualities of interaction that children enjoy in such natural learning contexts.
- Perceived problems such as lack of attention or lack of motivation are often the outcomes of a narrow focus that looks at language alone. So the more meaningful and challenging the language learning experience is for the learners, the more engaged they will be, and the more able to focus their attention.
- Rhythm and rhyme, images and imaginative thinking, story thinking and small talk are important cognitive tools. They play a key role in the child's learning of the new language.
- Scaffolding is one of the most important teacher interventions when working with very young learners. A child will be able to say on their own tomorrow what they are able to say with the teacher's help today.
- Very young children learn grammar naturally, through hearing new structures in natural contexts, and then imitating, noticing, remembering and trying to apply them.
- Errors are natural learning phenomena, and need to be viewed as such.
- In addition to having a solid level of linguistic and methodological competence, the teacher of very young learners needs to have an awareness of the learning and developmental opportunities that the shared space of the classroom offers, thus being an educator as much as a language teacher.

In conclusion, teaching very young learners is about being sensitive to the needs and development of the whole child. It involves providing routines and activities in a meaningful and engaging way within a safe, structured and learning-centred environment. Using accessible but natural language and the appropriate scaffolding techniques, we can guide our children towards producing language appropriate for their conversational needs.

We encourage you to practise becoming aware and present in the classroom. We hope the activities in this book will delight you as well as your very young learners … and we wish you well on your journey.

References

Egan, K. (1997) *The Educated Mind: How Cognitive Tools Shape Our Understanding*, University of Chicago Press.

Peccei, Jean Stilwell (1999) *Child Language*, Routledge.

Piaget, J. (2001) *The Language and Thought of the Child*, Routledge Classics.

Vygotsky, L. S. and Kozulin, A. (2012) *Thought and Language*, The MIT Press.

Wood, D., Bruner, J., & Ross, G. (1976) 'The role of tutoring in problem solving', in *Journal of Child Psychology and Child Psychiatry*, 17, pp.89–100.

Further reading

Early child development:

Bodrova, E. and Leong, D. J. (2007) *Tools of the Mind: The Vygotskian Approach to Early Childhood Education*, Pearson Education.

Egan, K. (1988) *Primary Understanding: Education in Early Childhood*, Routledge.

Egan K. (1999) *Teaching as Story Telling: An Alternative Approach to Teaching and Curriculum in the Elementary School*, University of Chicago Press.

Early second language acquisition:

Birdsong, D. (ed.) (1999) *Second Language Acquisition and the Critical Period Hypothesis*, Lawrence Erlbaum Associates.

Granena, G. and Long, M. (eds.) (2013) *Sensitive Periods, Language Aptitude and Ultimate L2 Attainment*, John Benjamins.

Herschensohn, J. (2007) *Language Development and Age*, Cambridge University Press.

Montrul, S. A. (2008) *Incomplete Acquisition in Bilingualism. Re-examining the Age Factor*, John Benjamins.

Nikolov, M. and Djigunovic, J. M. (2006) 'Recent Research on Age, Second Language Acquisition, and Early Foreign Language Learning', in *Annual Review of Applied Linguistics*, pp. 234–260.

Language teaching methodology:

Cameron, L. (2001) *Teaching Languages to Young Learners*, Cambridge University Press.

Lightbown, P. M. and Spada, N. (2013) *How Languages are Learnt*, 4th edition, Oxford University Press.

Puchta, H. and Williams, M. (2011) *Teaching Young Learners to Think. ELT activities for young learners aged 6 – 12*, Cambridge University Press and Helbling Languages.

Thornbury, S. 'The Learning Body' in Arnold, J. and Murphey, T. (2013) *Meaningful Action: Earl Stevick's Influence on Language Teaching*, pp. 62–78, Cambridge University Press.

Tips for teaching very young learners

1   Lesson planning

Lesson planning is always important, but it is essential when teaching very young children, since this age group requires a wide variety of short activities. Children will get bored if activities take too long and without necessarily meaning to, will start to disrupt your class. Get them standing and moving, then sitting and singing, then moving again. Craft activities will also keep children involved. Try to provide individual and group working and playing time within the lesson. Encourage good interaction but also independent endeavour.

Your lesson plan helps you to keep track of the order in which you are going to do all these things, as well as giving you a place to jot down extra information you may need to keep in mind for an activity you are presenting for the first time. You can also make a note of materials you will be using at each stage of your lesson. Finally, planning gives you an idea of the time each activity will take.

Tips:

- **Think about the main topic of your lesson and what you want to achieve.** Think about what you hope children will have learned by the end of the lesson. This is sometimes called the 'aim' of the lesson. Will your class learn new words (e.g. *cat, lion*), a new concept (e.g. pets vs wild animals) or how to use a structure (e.g. *A cat's small. A lion's big*)?
- **Keep to the same basic routine in every lesson.** With very young learners, routine is very important. Knowing what comes next will help children remember the language they need to fulfil each task. Use the routine that works for you – some teachers always start with a story, for instance.
- **Think about the way the whole lesson works.** When writing your lesson plan, try to see the flow of your lesson in your mind's eye, like a film director going through a script, imagining the various scenes of a film he or she is planning. Think of how each activity fits into the overall sequence. Is it a good fit? If not, would it fit better somewhere else in the sequence or would a different activity be better? As you write your lesson plan, you are likely to see a natural progression.
- **Plan 'transitions' between activities, as well as the main points of your lesson.** See Chapter 1, *Class routines and classroom management*, for activities to help you move from one step of the lesson to the next. Write down the activities you are planning but also note the main language you will need to use and anything that will help you present your ideas.
- **Be flexible.** You may not have time to do all the activities or steps you've planned. You may sometimes need to change the order of the lesson stages to suit what you are doing on a particular day (you might decide to start with a craft activity, for example, making puppets, so that children can use the puppets to participate during story time).
- **Have your materials ready.** Remember to set up the song you need so it is ready on the CD player or computer, or have your *Hello* slide on the interactive whiteboard when children come in.
- **Think about the lesson when it has finished.** Use a section of your lesson plan to write down ideas and reminders for the next class and to highlight things that went well or areas you need to work on.

Here is a possible order every lesson could follow:

Warmer: Begin your lesson with a 'hello' routine (see, for example, 1.1. Name tags: *Who's here today?* (page 32). When everyone has arrived, make a circle and perform the *Hello, how are you?* chant (1.5, page 36).

Circle time: Move on to routine activities, for example, talking about the date or the weather, phonics work or revising topic vocabulary. Use the board, charts, chants, songs, flashcards and question and answer techniques.

Story: Tell a story, generally related to the topic / craft activity or game which follows (see Chapter 4 *Stories and storytelling*). The story might be from a picture book or it could be a short film, puppet show or theatre activity, encouraging children's participation.

Topic / Craft: The children do this activity in groups at their tables. It can be based on the day's focus (taken from the story or the vocabulary topic, for example). See Chapter 5 *Arts, crafts and displays* and Chapters 6 and 7 for ideas.

Game or TPR: Do a get up and move activity, play a game or perform an action story with the children (see Chapter 2 *Movement and games*).

Wrap up: Finish the lesson with a settling activity, such as *What did we do today?* (1.14, page 49), followed by a 'goodbye' routine, for example, performing the *Goodbye chant* (1.15, page 50).

See the next page for a lesson plan template.

Lesson plan

Class: ....   Date: ....

Topic: ....

Aims: ....

....

Stage and time	What	Materials
1. Warmer Time:		
2. Circle time Time:		
3. Story Time:		
4. Topic / craft Time:		
5. Game Time:		
6. Wrap up Time:		

Post-lesson notes: ....
....
....
....
....

2   Starting the lesson

At the beginning of each class, children may seem 'far away' from English because they have probably been using only their own language since your last lesson. You need to help them to reconnect with the English language as fast and efficiently as possible. There are various ways for you to activate their prior knowledge and remind them that they are in a learning environment.

Tips:

- **Create a positive learning atmosphere from the very beginning of the class.** Establish that the language of the lesson is English by talking to the children as they enter the classroom, e.g. *Maria! Welcome back! So good to see you again. … Are you OK, Mario? Yes? That's good to hear. … Oh, you've got something in English on your T-shirt, Sandy. What does it say? …* Don't forget to smile at the children. Getting down to their level, so that you are face to face as you speak, will make them feel welcome and safe as they arrive.
- **Have something ready for children to do.** If you have regular latecomers or need to deal with jackets and bags when the children come in, prepare a simple activity for the other children to do at each table. If children are allowed to 'run wild' when they come in, it can affect their behaviour for the rest of the lesson. The activity you choose should be something the children have done before and that can be easily tidied away once completed. Examples are: 7.2 Sorting (page 175) or 7.7 Recognizing shapes: puzzles (page 182).
- **Signal the start of the class.** Use a clear signal to tell the class that it's time to start the lesson, for example, clap your hands and say *It's time to start the class, everyone.* Ask the children to tidy away the items on their tables, if they have been doing puzzles or sorting, e.g. *Put the pieces in the box. That's right Emma, in the box! Well done!*
- **Use a routine activity, song or chant to settle the children down.** To get the children in the right mood for learning, use a song or chant they are very familiar with, such as 1.7 The circle time chant (page 39).
- **Activate the English children already know.** Get the children thinking about what they did in the last lesson or review the topic vocabulary they have been learning. One way to do this is by word brainstorming. Say, for example, *Give me words from the last lesson. / Give me words from the story about Alice. / Give me four words for food. / Give me four numbers / colours.* Alternatively, review familiar instructions: ask a child to come to the front and give an instruction to a classmate (e.g. *Gary, clap your hands.*). That child stands up, carries out the instruction, gets a round of applause for getting it right, then swaps places with the child at the front and gives the next instruction to a different child.

3   The teacher's toolkit

Every teacher of very young learners needs an array of materials at hand. Preparing a 'teacher's toolkit' will mean you can always find the things you need at the right moment. We suggest you store all of your materials in a simple box with your name on it and take it with you to each lesson. You are sure to need at least one item from it, suddenly and without warning, in almost every class. Review your toolkit often and keep it refreshed to match changes in your class topic or the new songs / stories your children are learning.

Look in your toolkit when you are planning your lesson, as you will find some of the materials you need are already there (e.g. topic flashcards, the song CD, your storybook for the week). You can also use some of the items in your toolkit at the end of the lesson to review what the children have done (see also 1.14 *What did we do today?*, page 49).

Tools to include:
- **A pen and notepad**
- **Board pens** – Keep a mini whiteboard in the toolkit with the pens, if possible.
- **Flashcards** – It is useful to keep them in a plastic envelope or folder.
- **CDs**
- **Your current story**
- **Sticky tack or sellotape** – Sticky tack in particular seems to be one of those things you can never find when you most need it (it must be able to move of its own accord in the night). Among other uses, it's essential for displaying topic posters and children's work and playing flashcard games.
- **Scissors, glue stick, hole-punch** – These are not only vital for craft activities, but also for making and repairing items such as name tags.
- **Materials for your 'birthday routine'**, for example, a cardboard crown, birthday cake and candles (see 1.6 *Celebrating birthdays*, page 38).
- **An example of a finished craft item** if you are making something with your class that day.
- **Sticky notes** – You can use these for writing reminders, making observations during the class (see Tip 8 *Observation techniques*, page 27), playing games or as bookmarks.
- **Stickers** – These might be topic-related (animals, shapes) or reward stickers (stars, smiley faces).
- **Apron**

4   Classroom management

There are well-known techniques which encourage children to listen, to participate, to use their minds and to cooperate with their classmates. When children master the combination of listening and participating appropriately in the classroom, it is known as being *on task*. One of our most important roles as teachers is to encourage the kinds of behaviour that develop young children's learning skills. Another, of course, is giving them the freedom to play, to be and to explore who they are in a safe environment. Therefore, the core value of classroom management is guidance rather than discipline or punishment.

Developing our classroom management skills comes with practice and is a never-ending process, as new and inventive methods to motivate our children come to light. One thing we do know is that everyone responds to positive feedback and that giving children a clear idea of what they need to do in a happy and relaxed manner is the best way to help children become great learners. As well as the tips below, see Chapter 1 *Class routines and classroom management* for more ideas.

Tips:
- **Have a well thought-out lesson plan.** This is the best preparation for good classroom management (see Tip 1 *Lesson planning*, page 16).
- **Think about where your children will be sitting to avoid disruptions.** Certain combinations of children seem to work better than others. You may find that some children annoy each other if they sit together in circle time or for table activities. Once you've identified these combinations, separate the children in question by putting their name tags on different tables or by sitting them with other children at circle time.
- **Praise children for 'being good' and point them out as a model to show the others what they should be doing.** Give clear instructions, catch the children who quickly carry them out and comment on it, e.g. *Right everyone, it's story time. Sit and listen. What are we doing? We're sitting and listening. Oh well done, Charlie! That's great sitting and great listening. What about you, Delia? Can you sit like Charlie? Oh that's great. And thank you, Ahmed. What nice sitting! Let's start.*
- **Have paper or sticky notes and a pen handy to write down any positive or negative behaviour you observe.** Some children find it easier to be on task than others. Make a note of the differences among children (see Tip 8 *Observation techniques*, page 27). Some children are on task when doing crafts, for example, but don't cooperate so well during circle time.
- **Teach a particular posture to help children sit still.** When children are poking and pulling at each other or distracting classmates, ask them to sit in a familiar posture. For example, use gestures and say *Hands on heads, hands on knees, cross your arms … That's right, John. Very good. Cross your arms. That's right, you too, Milly. Well done!*
- **Have a technique for transitions, encouraging good behaviour before moving to a new activity.** For example, wait until children are sitting down and listening before you move them to their tables for a craft activity. Name the children who are ready and let only those children move, e.g. *We're going to make this dragon now, isn't that great? But stop! First, good sitting and listening, please. … Look at Jules! Great sitting. You can stand up and go to the table. Can you sit like Sophia, Gregor? Oh, that's great. Thank you. Sophia and Gregor, go to the tables!*

- **Use chants to get children's attention**, e.g. *One, two, three* (count with your fingers), *hands up* (put your hand up and wait for children to do the same) *and look at me* (point to yourself).
- **Use 'time outs' sparingly to help a misbehaving child calm down.** If a child is overexcited or disruptive, you may wish to give him or her a 'time out'. The child sits by him / herself, away from the rest of the class. Three things to remember about this technique are: a) it is often you who needs time out from the child, b) it is never the child we are punishing, but the behaviour we are addressing and c) for this age group, 'time out' should be a very short period of time (less than a minute). The aim is simply to give the child a little time alone to calm down before they rejoin the group.
- **Always make it clear why you are unhappy with a child's behaviour.** For example, if you are giving a 'time out', calmly explain the reasons to the child, e.g. *Adrian, I asked you to sit here because you are not working well with the other children. Please listen and look. Can you do that? Listen? Look at me? Thank you. Now come and join us!*
- **Use a star chart to help children recognize good behaviour.** Draw two lines horizontally on a piece of A3 paper to divide the paper into thirds. Draw a smiley face in the top third of the paper. Display the chart high up on a wall or noticeboard. Make a yellow paper star for each child. Write a child's name on each star and stick them in the middle section of the A3 paper with sticky tack.

  When a child is behaving in a way that brings harmony to the class, move their star to the section of the paper with the smiley face on it. Move the stars for children who are being disruptive down to the bottom third of the paper. Use this chart as you would play a game. Actively look for reasons to move children up, making sure to pay attention to quiet children (e.g. *Thank you for helping, Julien! Up you go!* (moving the star up on the chart)…). Use the chart to help the children who often need extra support to manage their behaviour, e.g. *Oh! Stewart! We're sitting listening to the story but you're running. Down you go. …* (moving the star down on the chart) *Oh that's better! OK! Here's your star next to the happy face.* (moving the star back up) *Well done!*

  Never move stars in anger and try to smile and stay calm. Remember to start every class with all the stars in the middle section of the chart.
- **Deal with interruptions quickly.** Sometimes a child will want your attention when you are working with the whole class. The reason for interrupting will always seem important to the child. If it is (e.g. they need to go to the bathroom or they are upset) deal with the situation immediately. You may even have to stop the class to resolve the issue.

  However, when a child wants to tell you about their baby brother, a visit to the park or some other matter, the rest of the class is likely to become distracted. For these kinds of interruptions, pull out your notepad and write the child's name down. Tell the child *That's very interesting. Yes, we'll talk about it later.* Show your notepad and say *Here's your name. Tell me later.* You may even be able to use some of the incidental information children tell you to involve them in an activity later in the lesson: *Guess what? Alba has a new dog! What's your dog's name? Well, here's a story about a pet. It's a very strange pet …*

5   Storytelling with picture books

Stories are important for young children on so many levels (see the introduction to Chapter 4 *Stories and storytelling*, page 89). If you choose your story well and recognize the points where children need help to follow the plot and encourage participation, children will join in with enthusiasm.

Tips:

- **Choose the story carefully.** Look for storybooks with large, colourful pictures that can be seen and enjoyed by the whole class. Consider the level of the language in the book, think how the story fits with your topic and about activities you can do to extend and practise the language. Make sure you choose stories with endings that don't rely on understanding difficult ideas.
- **Read the story first.** Note any words or concepts which children might find difficult. See how much vocabulary can be taught using the cover of the book and the first page of the story.
- **Plan your actions.** Think of mimes and gestures to explain actions, concepts or emotions.
- **Keep pre-teaching of new words to a minimum.** Draw pictures, use flashcards or real objects to teach no more than six key words from the story before you tell it. Try not to prolong this step, as teaching vocabulary is not the aim of the activity.
- **Clearly mark the start of the story.** Start by saying *It's story time*. Expect children to sit quietly during the telling of the story (see Activity 1.9 the *Listen, please* chant, page 43).
- **Show the cover of the book first.** Talk about the cover picture and use it to introduce the characters and generate interest, e.g. *What's this? Yes, it's the sun. It's a sunny day. What's this? It's a bear.*
- **Tell children the title of the story and the author's name.** Trace the title of the story with your finger as you say, e.g. *Harry's birthday, by …*
- **Hold the book so everyone can see each page.** If you're using a small book, hold it at the bottom so that you have one hand free to turn the pages and point. If you're using a big book, prop it on a chair and stand beside it. This leaves your hands free to turn the pages, point, make gestures or mime.
- **Use different voices for the different characters in the story.** Alter your voice to show who is speaking, for example, use a high voice for a baby bear and a deep voice for a big bear.
- **Use varying tone and pitch.** When you tell the story, you can whisper or speak very quietly when something is about to happen, in order to add atmosphere.
- **Encourage participation.** Give the children plenty of opportunities to join in or repeat key phrases. They can also copy your mimes for the feelings of the characters and act out the story.
- **When telling stories using a book, before turning the page, ask the children to make a prediction.** For example, gesture that you are about to turn the page and say *There's a snake: 'yes', 'no' or 'I don't know'?* If some children think they know the answer, they may say *yes* or *no* and this is perfectly acceptable. At the same time, we're giving our children a valuable new phrase (*I don't know*), to use when they are unsure of an answer.
- **Clearly mark the end of the story.** When the story's over, say *And that's the story of ….* This brings the storytelling to a close and if children enjoyed the story they may even clap or say *Again!*
- **Let children look at the storybook themselves.** Put the book in a special place in the classroom with an *Our Storybook* sign. Encourage children to look at the book on their own.
- **Make an *Our Story* display** with the key vocabulary and phrases from the story.
- **Use the story as the basis for a project.** For example, after telling *Jack and the Beanstalk*, grow plants from seeds.

6 Organizing and giving instructions for craft activities

Most children adore craft activities and they will happily and busily get to work without feeling self-conscious or afraid. The success of a craft activity in the English language classroom often lies in giving clear instructions and we must also make sure that there is enough language input. This includes asking children to help, giving them choices about the materials they want to use, asking them questions about what they are making and giving plenty of positive feedback on their creations.

Tips:

- **Choose a craft activity that links to the topic of the lesson.** Try to find an activity that ties in with a story you have told or the vocabulary set you are teaching.
- **Think about each step in the project.** Make sure you have all the materials for the different steps.
- **Plan your instructions.** For each step of the activity, think about how you will explain what the children have to do and how to use the different materials.
- **Show the children an example of what they will be making.** Make the item before the class. Set the scene for your craft activity before children go to their tables. Say, e.g. *Today we're going to make magic wands.* Hold up the item you've made and let the children pass it around.
- **Use helpers to distribute and collect materials.** Make sure everyone gets a turn as a helper.
- **Demonstrate each step before distributing the materials children need.** Once they have craft materials in front of them, children will be busy cutting, painting or sticking rather than paying attention to your instructions.
- **Only give children the material(s) they need for each step.** This avoids confusion and extra clutter.
- **Clean up as much as possible between steps.** This will help the children to see what step they are at in the project and it will save work at the end of the lesson. Say, for example, *Now let's put the paper in the bin. OK. Now Henry's going to collect the scissors. June's going to give you the glue.*
- **Accept a certain level of noise and chat.** Allow for an appropriate level of noise and for children speaking in their own language while they are working. However, move around the class and interact with individual children while this is happening. Ask questions with simple one-word or short answers, e.g. *What colour do you need? Green? How many circles to you want?*
- **Stop the activity if necessary to give more instructions.** If you need everyone's attention, use a chant, e.g. *One, two, three, hands up and look at me* or *Hands on heads and look at me.* If children have paintbrushes or scissors in their hands, say, e.g. *Put your scissors down on the table.* before you say the chant. Once you have their attention, give the next set of instructions.
- **Give lots of praise and encouragement.** Enjoy your children's creations and the excitement making them brings. Try to find something different or special about each child's work to comment on, and make sure you ask questions, e.g. *Great! That's a lovely dog, Vera. Has it got a name?*
- **Make sure children know what to do when they have finished.** And make sure their names are on their work! With the smallest ones, this could mean that you write their names on the craft item as they're making it; with older children, try to get them to write their names on their work at the beginning. If the items the class have made need to dry, get the children to hang them on a clothesline with pegs or put them on a drying rack. Take time to look at and comment on everyone's work.

- Give each child a large paper or plastic plate at the beginning of the year with their name on it. Children use the plate throughout the year to paint and construct their creations on. The plates are also handy for keeping crafts separate until they're finished.
- **Display work before children take it home.** Show children their art display in the next class. Talk about their work. Use this as an opportunity to revise language connected to the project, e.g. *What did we make? Shapes towns! Here's Bernard's town. Look at the house! What colour is it? Is it your house, Bernard? Wow! What great towns we made!*

7   Using songs, stories and games from the internet

There's a wealth of resources on the internet for very young learners of English, but there are also problems with using these resources. Not every story, song or game you find will be appropriate, and you could find yourself spending far too much time searching for a few minutes' worth of class material.

Tips:

- **Choose material carefully.** When looking for songs, short stories or games online, consider the children's language level, whether the material suits the topic of your lesson and whether it will appeal to the age group. Avoid spending hours using search engines by asking colleagues to recommend good educational websites.
- **Check the material.** Make sure you watch the song or story or play the game in its entirety. Note any key language or concepts you might have to pre-teach in order for the material to work in your class. Ensure that whatever you are going to use is appropriate and check the advertising content (occasionally adverts will appear in the middle of a story or game, in which case you will have to discard it). You could suggest your centre install advert-blocking software.
- **Assign the material a place in your lesson.** Is it a good way to start your class, e.g. a *How are you?* song? Would it add to your circle time? If the activity involves playing a game or a lot of movement, it might be better placed after circle time or at the end of the lesson.
- **Set up in advance.** Make sure you have all the equipment you need (e.g. computer, remote control, IWB, projector). Prepare the clip or game by skipping any advertisements and pausing right at the beginning. Minimize the website / application and have it ready at the bottom of the screen to pull up at the right point in your lesson.
- **Be prepared for technical problems.** Have a back-up song, story or game ready which does not require the computer, in case you encounter technical problems.

8   Observation techniques

Keeping a record of your children's performance helps you to create a reliable picture of their progress. The records you create by dedicating time to observing individuals in class are invaluable. You can use them during parent–teacher consultations or if you have a particular issue you need to discuss with a parent. Parents will appreciate concrete instances of good or challenging behaviour, examples of the language their child knows or evidence to substantiate any concerns you have.

Tips:

- **Keep observation notes in the same place.** Have a section at the back of your notebook for writing down observations.
- **Choose the best time to observe the children.** This is when children are working independently or in small groups. You may of course want to write a quick note at other times when you notice a particular behaviour or when a learning issue arises.
- **Use sticky notes during classes.** You might not have time to write complete notes during a lesson, so you can jot down observations on notes. After the class, stick the notes with your observations for the child in question.

Below are some examples:

> Alba is making her own town while the others are building the town around the street.

> Gorka said, 'I don't like fish,' without any prompting.

> Hugo is helping Greta to put the correct number of beans into the numbered pots.

Your notes are likely to be shorter than these – they will contain just enough information for you to remember what you noticed. Don't try to take more than three notes per class.

- **Make sure you take notes about positive as well as challenging moments.** For example, if you see a child helping others, showing progress or using English in a particularly interesting way, jot it down. You may have the opportunity to communicate these moments to parents.
- **Observe everyone.** Check your notes to see which children are not generating many observation points (these are often the quieter ones). Make an effort to observe these children in the next class.
- **Ask a colleague to help you.** If you have an assistant, ask them to take some notes. They may be freer than you to observe children during teacher-led activities.

9   Involving parents

The role of the parent in a child's education is fundamental to their success, so make sure to keep parents informed of your class activities and topics, as well as their child's individual progress.

Your children's parents or carers are important allies. Their attitudes towards their children's language learning will influence the children's own beliefs and motivation. This is why it is good to meet the parents at the beginning of the year and also to discuss progress with them throughout the year. You can involve parents in their children's learning in a simple and informative way by sending home a regular letter explaining what you are doing in class. You will find an example layout for the letter on the next page.

Tips:

- **At your first meeting with parents / carers, explain that you'll send home a letter with a summary of what you've done in class.** In this way, parents will know the topics, stories and songs you've covered. You can choose how regularly to send the letter (e.g. weekly or monthly).
- **Include the main topics, songs or stories in your letter.** You do not need to add everything you have done in every lesson. The content of the letter should enable parents to ask their children questions and give ideas for fun 'homework' that parents and children can share.
- **Provide links to any online material,** such as songs you've learned or games you've played in class so that children can revise at home. Parents particularly enjoy the experience of listening to their children singing English songs. If you send the letter as an email, you can easily add such links and even attach short video clips of the class that you record during the lessons (make sure you have all the parents' permission to do this beforehand).
- **You may want to include a 'special tip'.** Examples could include: 'Errors are signs of learning. Nobody can learn without making mistakes.' 'Your child learns the new language by doing things, for example, action stories or craft activities.'
- **If using paper copies, hand out the letters when children are ready to go home.** Older children can put their letters in their bags. As you hand out the letter, say *This is for Mummy and Daddy. Give it to them when you get home.*
- **Parents who don't speak English should still be able to understand the categories in the letter,** and they will also be able to share an English experience with their child, if you include internet links. You may wish to translate the letter into the children's own language if you're able to, or translate topic names in brackets, for example, *Topic: clothes (ropa).* However, we have found that most parents like receiving the letter in English.
- **Ask parents to discuss the English lessons with their children.** Suggest they start with small questions, e.g. *Was there a birthday today? Who did you sit with? What did you make?* instead of expecting the child to describe everything they did in the lesson.

Child's name: _____	Date: _____
Teacher: _____	Our topic this week / month is _____ .
Assistant: _____	We made _____ and
	played a game called _____ .
Please watch 'The ___ Song' with your child. Website:	Stories: _____ _____
Special tip:	

Figure 0.1: Example layout for a letter to parents / carers

1   Class routines and classroom management

One of the biggest challenges facing teachers of very young learners is capturing and maintaining the attention of our students, when some are more interested in other things happening in the classroom than in the activities we have carefully prepared for them.

There is no doubt that class routines help children to stay focused and make them feel safe. Most of us establish routines in our daily lives, simply because they allow us to get more done and give us a sense of achievement. This is no different in a lesson for young learners and is all the more important when they are learning a foreign language. Exposing very young children to familiar phrases with an obvious outcome, for example, before listening to a story or when it's time to tidy up, serves to increase the amount of English they are hearing and producing, in an authentic way.

Children will understand what is being said by knowing what is expected of them at most (but not all!) times. That is why we've included activities which establish routines and provide ways to transition from one part of the lesson to another in the very first chapter of this book. The chapter describes ways to start and end the lesson, ways to signal new phases of the lesson and activities to create calm or to provide a change of pace.

Although we must be open to straying from our plans, so that learning can take place at any opportunity, a lack of routine can lead to loss of control and the sense that time is being wasted. When this happens, it's important to have techniques for bringing the class back on task or moving to the next stage of the lesson. Chants are a great way to do this. They require no preparation or supporting material and once children have learned them, they're immediately speaking English.

You will notice that we've included suggestions for lots of gestures and optional flashcards with the activities in this chapter. This is because for this age group and level, visual reminders are important for understanding the language and developing positive classroom behaviour.

You can pick and choose from the ideas presented here, depending on your preferences and classroom situation, as it would be impossible to use all the activities in one class! Experiment with different activities and modify them until you find a routine that works best for you.

1.1 Name tags: *Who's here today?*

Outline	Children find their name tag and display it on a *Who's here today?* poster.
Focus	*What's your name? I'm ... Where's your name tag? Who's here today?*
Age	3–7
Time	2–5 minutes, depending on class size
Materials	An A3 piece of cardboard, a piece of card for each child in your class (to make a name tag), a square of different coloured card, sticky tack.
Preparation	Make a poster from A3 card with the title *Who's here today?* Display the poster on the wall at a height children can reach. Make a name tag for each child and put sticky tack on the back.

Procedure

1 Place the children's name tags in random order on the wall near the entrance to the classroom or on the teacher's desk / children's tables.

2 In the first few classes, as each child enters the classroom ask *What's your name?* and give out the correct name tag or help the child to find it. The child sticks their name tag on the *Who's here today?* poster.

3 As children become familiar with the activity, they find their own name tag, without your help, as they arrive. While the children are looking for their name tags say, for example, *Where's your name tag, Maria? Look around. Can you see it? Yes! There it is. Well done! Have you got your name tag, Cristina? Show me your name tag, please. Is it this one? No – it says Carlos. Here it is.*

4 When children have stuck their name tags on the poster, sit them down in a circle. Ask *Who's here today?* and use the poster as a register.

5 Put the name tags for any children who are absent to the side of the poster or place them on the different coloured square of card.

Variations

1 For three year-olds who can't yet read their names, put photos on the tags and give them more assistance. Four year-olds may need help to find their written name tags at first.

2 Include name tags for you and any other regular adult members of class.

3 Give your poster and tags a theme to help create a group identity (see 1.2 Create a group identity: *We are stars!*).

4 Glue the name tags to pegs. The children peg their name tags on a *Who's here today?* clothes line. When they have work to display, the children can also hang it from their name tag.

5 Turn the name tags into pendants, using a hole punch and string. Children wear them for the first few lessons, so you can remember their names. Alternatively, use double-sided tape to stick the tags to their clothes.

Note

Cover the poster with sticky-backed plastic and laminate the name tags so they last longer.

1.2 Create a group identity: *We are stars!*

Outline	Children find their name star, display it on a sky poster and perform a chant to begin the class.
Focus	*Who's here today? Where's your star? We are …, stars, high, sky, fantastic, strong*
Age	3–7
Time	5–10 minutes, depending on class size
Materials	Dark blue cardboard (to represent the night sky), a star made of card for each child in your class (to make a name tag), sticky tack.
Preparation	Make a night sky poster from cardboard. Display the poster on the wall at a height children can reach. You could give it the title *We are stars!* Write each child's name on a star and put sticky tack on the back. A star template can be found on the website. Listen to the chant on the website.

Procedure

1 Place the star name tags in random order on the wall near the entrance to the classroom or on the teacher's desk / children's tables.

2 When the children enter the classroom at the start of class, they find their star and put it on the night sky poster. See the Procedure for Activity 1.1. for language to use at this stage.

3 When all the stars are in the sky, say *Let's make a circle*. The children stand in a circle, holding hands. They all say the following chant and do the actions (in brackets):

We are stars!	(let go of each other's hands and point to selves)
We are high,	(lift hands above heads and wriggle fingers)
In the sky!	(wave hands high above heads)
We're fantastic!	(jump in the air, arms outstretched)
And we are strong,	(make fists and lift arms in a 'strong' gesture)
We are strong!	(repeat 'strong' gesture)

Variations

1 Three year-olds perform the gestures of the chant only, older children join in with the whole chant.

2 Children make their own stars at the beginning of the school year. Ask younger children to colour a star shape and trace over or write their name. Teach older children to draw their own five-pointed star to cut out and colour.

Note

Once children have placed the stars in the sky to show who's here, you can use them on a behaviour management chart (see Teacher's tip 4: Classroom management *Use a star chart to help children recognize good behaviour*, page 22).

> ### ♀ Tip
>
> Participating in an activity such as this at the beginning of every lesson helps to create a group identity. It provides children with a sense of belonging, so that they feel safe and special, encouraging them to learn and share. You may prefer another theme, for example, tiger name tags on a jungle poster or bee name tags on flowers.

1.3 A starting class routine

Outline	Children draw pictures of known items while others are arriving in class.
Focus	Revision of nouns
Age	4–7
Time	5–10 minutes
Materials	Paper and crayons or mini-whiteboards and markers.
Preparation	Draw a simple picture of one or more items children know on the board, e.g. classroom objects, an animal, a tree, a flower, a type of food or a mode of transport. Place crayons / whiteboard markers in one box and paper / whiteboards in another. Put the boxes on a table or on the floor close to the children's seating area.

Procedure

1 As children enter the classroom, tell them to go to the boxes and take a piece of paper and a crayon (or a mini-whiteboard and a marker).

2 Show your picture on the board and ask the children to copy it on their paper or whiteboard. Say, e.g. *What's this? Is it a tree? Look here's my crayon and paper. Can you see? I'm drawing a tree. Can you draw a tree?* Once some children have started, others entering the room will know what to do.

3 Talk about the children's pictures as they draw, e.g. *That's a beautiful tree! Can you colour it? Oh look! You've put a smiley face in your circle, Ana. Are you happy today? What a big bus! Do you like buses, Sergio?*

4 When the children have finished drawing and you are ready to move on to the next stage of the lesson, say *Well done everyone! I can see your (tree and flower).*

5 Children write their names on their pictures or clean the whiteboards and put them in the box. They tidy up the crayons / markers.

Variations

1 For three year-olds, provide a box of toys for children to play with as they arrive instead of drawing materials (e.g. soft toy animals which children can name in English). As the children play, ask, e.g. *What have you got, Nora? Ah! A cat. You're playing with a cat. What colour is it?*

2 Older children can copy a word you have written on the board and draw a picture to go with it.

Extension ideas

• If they have drawn on paper, children continue their pictures at the start of the next class. You could add more items to your board drawing for them to copy or let them use their imagination.

• Display the pictures or show them in circle time. Use pictures of different objects to revise and develop language skills, e.g. *Look at Mario's picture. What is it? Yes, it's a beautiful yellow bus. Now who did this butterfly? Did you draw it Paul? It's very good!*

Note

Keep your own drawing simple and clear to make sure the activity doesn't take too long.

1.4 The *What's your name?* bean bag chant

Outline	Children throw a bean bag to each other while performing a chant, to help them learn their classmates' names.
Focus	*What's your name? I'm (Alba)*.
Age	3–7
Time	2–5 minutes, depending on class size
Materials	A bean bag (one for each group).
Preparation	None

Procedure

1 Say *Let's make a circle*. The children stand in a circle. If you have a large class and an assistant, make two circles.

2 Stamp your feet three times and say *What's your name? What's your name?* Throw the bean bag in the air and catch it, then say your name *I'm…! I'm…!*

3 Stamp your feet three times and say *What's your name? What's your name?* and throw the bean bag to a child. The child catches it and says their name, e.g. *I'm Alba! I'm Alba!*

4 Make a throwing gesture to show that the child needs to throw the bean bag to another child. At the same time everyone claps and says *What's your name? What's your name?*

5 Go around the circle until everyone has had a turn. You could use this activity to get the children ready for circle time.

Variation

With very young children use a simpler version of the chant. Say, e.g. *Hello, Bruno!* The rest of the class repeats *Hello, Bruno!* Pass the bean bag to Bruno. Say the name of the next child, e.g. *Hello, Sara!* The rest of the class repeats *Hello, Sara!* and Bruno passes the bean bag to Sara.

Notes

• Ask very young children to sit instead of stand, as they will be able to catch the bean bag more easily.

• If your class is very excitable, have children pass the bean bag in a clockwise direction around the circle, rather than throwing it.

1.5 The *Hello, how are you?* chant

Outline	Children perform a 'hello' chant.
Focus	*Hello, how are you today? I'm fine, thank you.*
Age	4–7
Time	5 minutes
Materials	Optional: *Hello, how are you?* chant flashcard (see page 37 or print from the website).
Preparation	Listen to the chant on the website.

Procedure

1 Say *Let's make a circle. It's time to say 'hello'.* The children stand in a circle.
2 Say the following chant. The children join in with the actions (in brackets). In time, children may also join in with the words.

Teacher:	*Hello, hello, hello!*	(wave)
Children:	*Hello, hello, hello!*	(wave)
Teacher:	*How are you today?*	(question gesture)
Children:	*I'm fine, thank you!*	(hold thumbs up)
Teacher:	*And I'm great, too!*	(hold hands up in the air)
Teacher:	*Are you ready for English?*	
Children:	*Yes!*	
All:	*Hooray!*	(everyone claps)

Variation
With very young children, change the words to:

Teacher:	*Hello, hello, hello!*
Children:	*Hello, hello, hello!*
Teacher:	*Are you ready for English?*
Children:	*Yes!*
All:	*Hooray!*

💡 **Tip**

Photocopy the flashcard on the next page, write the words of the chant on the back and laminate it. Hold up the flashcard to signal this stage in the lesson. Read the words from the back of the flashcard instead of reading from the book.

PHOTOCOPIABLE

1.6 Celebrating birthdays

Outline	The class celebrates a child's birthday.
Focus	Days of the week, months, numbers, *cake, candle, How old are you? Happy birthday! Make a wish!*
Age	4–7
Time	5 minutes
Materials	A picture of a cake (or draw a cake on the board), a candle (real, electric or homemade, e.g. from a straw and a yellow feather), a cardboard crown or party hat, a CD with birthday music. Optional: A 'birthday poster' showing the months of the year in English with the names of children whose birthdays fall in each month written on it, together with the dates; a birthday storybook.
Preparation	Write the date of each child's birthday on a poster or in your diary at the start of the year. At the beginning of each week, check if anyone has a birthday coming up and plan the celebration for the lesson on the nearest day.

Procedure

1 If you have a birthday poster on the wall, point to it at the beginning of the week and ask *Are there any birthdays this week?* Children are usually very excited about their birthdays, but some may not remember or will be too shy to tell you. Say, e.g. *Look! What's today? It's Tuesday and it's Irem's birthday.* Invite the birthday child to come to the front of the class.

2 Switch on your birthday music. If you have a birthday story, this is a good time to read it to create an atmosphere of celebration. Put the cardboard birthday crown or hat on the child's head and say *Happy birthday (Irem)!* The rest of the class repeat.

3 Hold up your picture of a cake and the candle or draw a cake with a candle on the board. Say *Make a wish! Blow the candle out!* Close your eyes as if you are making a wish then mime blowing the candle out.

4 The child closes their eyes and mimes blowing out the candle. Encourage the class to cheer *Hooray!* If you don't have a picture of a cake, erase the candles on the cake you have drawn on the board, when the birthday child pretends to blow them out.

Note

Everyone likes to be remembered on their birthday, but very young children become extremely excited about theirs, perhaps because they have celebrated so few and for them a year seems a long time. It is therefore a good idea to have a simple pre-prepared routine which allows you to make each child feel special on their birthday, without turning birthday celebrations into whole-lesson affairs.

💡 **Tip**

Celebrate with all the children who have birthdays in the holidays in one of the classes at the end of the term / year to make sure they don't miss out.

1.7 The circle time chant

Outline	Children perform a chant to get ready for sitting in a circle in class.
Focus	*Sit down! Hands up! Circle time, please.*
Age	3–7
Time	5 minutes
Materials	Optional: *Circle time* chant flashcard (see page 40 or print from the website).
Preparation	None

Procedure

1 Say *It's circle time*. Gesture for children to move to the circle time area, if you have one in your classroom. Move to your chair and make sure you have any materials you need for circle time.

2 Say the following chant. The children join in with the actions (in brackets). In time, children may also join in with the words.

Sit down, sit down,	(hold hands with palms flat facing the floor, pushing downwards)
Sit down, please.	(all sit down)
Hands up! Hands up!	(hold hands up in the air)
Hands up with me!	(repeat hands up action)
It's circle time.	(make a circle with your index finger, pointing downwards)
It's circle time.	(repeat the circle action)
So listen carefully!	(speak slowly and quietly, pointing to your ears)

Variations

1 If you have a big class and it takes a long time to get them settled, say *So sit down, please!* instead of *So listen carefully!* the first time you say the chant. Repeat the chant until everyone is sitting and then finish the last time with *So listen carefully!* Encourage a calm atmosphere by repeating the chant, more and more quietly. You could even whisper it the last time.

2 Children can take turns to start circle time by leading the chant, once the class has learned it.

> 💡 **Tip**
>
> Photocopy the flashcard on the next page, write the words of the chant on the back and laminate it. Hold up the flashcard to signal this stage in the lesson. Read the words from the back of the flashcard instead of reading from the book.

From *Activities for Very Young Learners* © Cambridge University Press 2017

1.8 A classical music routine

Outline	Children listen to a short piece of classical music and do calming exercises.
Focus	*hands, knees, shoulders, head, up, down, round, gently, like this, breathe, one, two, three*
Age	3–7
Time	2 minutes
Materials	A short extract of calming classical music, lasting around one minute (on computer / CD).
Preparation	Have the music ready to play.

Procedure

1 Ask the children to sit down. Switch on the music and say *Listen and follow me*.
2 Give the instructions below and do the actions (in brackets). The children listen and do the actions. It's easy if you remember the sequence *hands, shoulders, head*.

Put your hands out like this.	(stretch your arms out in front of you)
Hands up!	(move your hands up at the wrist, so that your palms are facing the children)
Hands down!	(move your down at the wrist, so that the backs of your hands are facing the children)
Hands up and down!	(repeat the hands up and down actions)
Hands round and round.	(move your hands around gently clockwise at the wrist in a circular motion)
Hands round and round.	(repeat the action counter-clockwise)
Put your hands on your knees.	(put your hands on your knees and leave them there for the rest of the routine)
Shoulders up!	(lift your shoulders up)
Shoulders down!	(put your shoulders down)
Shoulders up and down!	(repeat the shoulders up and down action)
Shoulders round and round.	(make gentle circular motions with your shoulders)
Shoulders round and round.	(repeat the circular motions in the other direction)
Now your head, gently, up and down.	(nod your head – make sure children do this gently)
And round and round.	(make a gentle circular motion with your head in both directions)
Now breathe … one … two … three.	(breathe in and out deeply three times)

Variations

1 Once children know the movements by heart, you can sit with the group and choose a different child to lead the exercises at the beginning of each lesson.

2 The sequence of movements above is just a suggestion. Do any movements you feel comfortable with. Another sequence you could include is:

One hand up.	(hold your right hand out, with the palm facing the ceiling)
Other hand up.	(hold your left hand out, with the palm facing the ceiling)
One hand on your shoulder.	(put your right palm on your left shoulder)
Other hand on your other shoulder.	(put your left palm on your right shoulder)
One hand on your knee.	(put your left hand on your left knee)
Other hand on your knee.	(put your right hand on your right knee)

Notes

- Make sure children move gently and follow your movements exactly, especially when using their heads.
- Keep in mind that there is a perfect pace for this activity. If it doesn't take too long, children will really enjoy it.
- If you use an interactive whiteboard, you could add a music icon and a link to the classical music on the appropriate slide (e.g. your circle time or story time slide).
- Karen learned the technique in this routine from Eli Redondo.

1.9 The *Listen, please* chant

Outline	Children perform a chant to get ready for listening.
Focus	*hands, heads, knees, Hands on (heads), Cross your arms, Listen, please.*
Age	3–7
Time	2 minutes
Materials	Optional: *Listen, please* chant flashcard (see page 44 or print from the website).
Preparation	Listen to the chant on the website.

Procedure

1 Use this chant whenever you want the class to sit quietly and pay attention (e.g. when you want to start a story, change to a new activity or give instructions).

2 Say the chant quietly and calmly. The children join in with the actions (in brackets). Once they know the chant, they may also join in with the words.

Hands on heads,	(put your hands on your head)
Hands on knees,	(put your hands on your knees)
Cross your arms,	(cross your arms)
And listen, please.	(put one hand to your ear)

Variations

1 When using the chant after art and craft activities, start by saying *Everything down now,* (demonstrate by putting some things you are holding on the table). Then continue with *Hands on heads … .*

2 Once children know the chant by heart, choose a volunteer to lead it.

3 Teach the children this shorter version:

One, two, three,	(count on your fingers)
Hands up!	(put your hand up in the air)
And look at me!	(point to yourself and make a gesture to mean 'quiet')

💡 Tips

1 With their arms crossed, children are less able to distract their classmates. Use the *Cross your arms* instruction separately when individual children need to be still.

2 Photocopy the flashcard on the next page, write the words of the chant on the back and laminate it. Hold up the flashcard to signal this stage in the lesson. Read the words from the back of the flashcard instead of reading from the book.

From *Activities for Very Young Learners* © Cambridge University Press 2017

1.10 The table time chant

Outline	Children perform a chant to get ready to sit at their tables.
Focus	*table time, draw, colour, write*
Age	3–7
Time	2 minutes
Materials	A pencil and a crayon.
Preparation	None

Procedure

1   Stand in front of the class and draw the shape of a table in the air or draw a picture of a table on the board.

2   Say the following chant rhythmically and do the actions (in brackets):

> *Table, table, table time!*
> *Table, table, table time!*

> | *Draw!* | (pick up a pencil and mime drawing) |
> |---|---|
> | *Colour!* | (pick up a crayon and mime colouring) |
> | *Write!* | (mime writing) |

3   Repeat the verbs (*draw, colour, write*) and the actions several times, encouraging the children to join in.

Variation

Once children know the chant by heart, you can extend it as follows:

> *Table, table, table time!*
> *Come with me.*

> | *Sit at the table* | (point at a table) |
> |---|---|
> | *And draw with me.* | (mime drawing) |

Change the last line of this version to fit the kind of activity you want the class to do, e.g. *Sit at the table ... And colour with me.* (mime colouring) or *Sit at the table ... And write with me.* (mime writing).

1.11 The story time chant

Outline	Children perform a chant to get them ready to listen to a story.
Focus	*It's story time. Oh, what fun! Look and listen.*
Age	3–7
Time	2–5 minutes
Materials	None
Preparation	None

Procedure

1 Stand still in front of your class for about 10 seconds. This will make the children curious. Move your lips as if speaking the following words, but do not say them aloud:

> *It's story time.*
> *It's story time.*

2 Gradually start whispering the words:

> *It's story time.*
> *It's story time.*

3 Say the words a little bit louder, but still in a very secretive manner:

> *It's story time.*
> *It's story time.*

4 Then say the whole chant with actions (in brackets). Encourage the children to join in with the actions. Once they know the chant, they may also join in with the words.

It's story time.	(mime opening a book, or point to your storybook)
It's story time.	(repeat the same action)
Oh, what fun!	(look enthusiastic)
Look and listen.	(point at your eyes and ears)
Three, two, one!	(count down from three to one on your fingers)

1.12 Let's move

Outline	Children move to an energizing chant.
Focus	*stand up, stretch, jump, hop, stop, up, down*
Age	3–7
Time	3–5 minutes
Materials	None
Preparation	None

Procedure

1 Ask the children to stand up. Say *It's time to move!* Then say the following chant and do the actions (in brackets):

Stand up and stretch!	(stand up and stretch your arms up in the air)
Stand up and jump!	(jump in the air)
Hop, jump, hop, jump!	(hop and jump)
Stop!	(stand very still)

2 Say the chant twice and finish by saying *Stop* more quietly the second time.

3 After this 'stirrer' activity, ask children to sit down and continue your lesson, or show the class where to go for the next activity.

Variation

Add different actions after *Stand up and jump* to make the chant longer:

Up, down, up, down	(stretch your arms up and then touch the ground)
Turn around!	(turn around on the spot)

Note

This is a good transition activity to use when the children have to move from one part of the room to another, or when they are getting restless and need a change of pace.

1.13 Let's tidy up

Outline	Children help to tidy up the classroom.
Focus	*Let's tidy up, please, Thank you, everyone. Good job! Nice tidying!* Instructions and prepositions, e.g. *Put the crayons in the box, Give the glue to …*
Age	3–7
Time	2–5 minutes
Materials	None
Preparation	None

Procedure

1 Start by speaking quietly, clapping as you say *Let's tidy up! Tidy up, tidy up, please.*

2 Add instructions and gestures to show children what they need to do, e.g. *Put the crayons in the box, please. Put your papers here, please.*

3 If you have helpers, say, e.g. *Give the glue to Kasia, please.*

4 Continue to quietly repeat these simple phrases until your classroom is tidy. Say *Thank you, everyone. Good job! Nice tidying!*

> **Tips**
>
> 1 It can be difficult to get children's attention when it's time to tidy up, especially after a colouring or craft activity. This shouldn't lead to you doing all the tidying up yourself, however, because teaching children to put things away is part of our responsibility.
>
> 2 Use clapping with any instructions as a way to get your children's attention, rather than raising your voice. It becomes a signal to help them recognize a change from one stage of the lesson to the next.

1.14 What did we do today?

Outline	Children think about and revise what they learned in the lesson.
Focus	*What was our story / song / chant? What words do we know?*, vocabulary from the lesson
Age	3–7
Time	2–5 minutes
Materials	A large cardboard box (you could decorate or paint it).
Preparation	None

Procedure

1   Put the things you use in the lesson (e.g. story book, flashcards of key words, craft materials or finished items) in the box as you finish with them.
2   At the end of the lesson, take the items out of the box in turn, show the children and ask questions. For example, hold up the story book and ask *What was our story today? … Harry's birthday!* Show flashcards of the vocabulary you have learned and ask, e.g. *What words did we learn today? That's right! It's an apple. We learned about fruit. What's this? An orange!* Hold up any materials you used for games and say, e.g. *Look! How many triangles? Six! Two big and four small ones. What shapes did you make with the triangles? A square and a rectangle! What else? A house and an arrow. Great!*
3   At the beginning of the next lesson, use the items from the box to remind children of their last class, e.g. hold up the story book again and ask *What was our story (yesterday)?*

Variation

Draw a picture representing a word the class have learned on the board, line by line. Ask *What is it?* as you draw, until someone guesses. Say the word. Everyone repeats. Do this for one or two more new words as children try to guess.

Extension idea

If you have your own classroom, you could have a permanent *What we did today* display shelf. Put flashcards of key words, the story book you're reading, craft items you have made and any other objects from topic activities on the shelf. Change the objects when your topic changes.

> ### 💡 Tip
>
> During the lesson, children are often very engaged in activities and yet not aware that they are actually learning. At the end of a class, showing objects from the lesson encourages children to become aware of their progress and provides an extra point of recall for key concepts, language and vocabulary.

1.15 The *Goodbye* chant

Outline	Children perform a 'Goodbye' chant at the end of the lesson.
Focus	*It's time to …, line up, say 'goodbye'*
Age	3–7
Time	2–5 minutes
Materials	Optional: The *Goodbye* chant flashcard (see page 51 or print from the website).
Preparation	Optional: This chant can be sung. Listen to the song on the website.

Procedure

1 Point to your watch or the clock or show the *Goodbye* chant flashcard. Say *Look! It's time to go.*
2 Say the following chant and do the actions (in brackets):

It's time, it's time, it's time,	(point to your watch or the clock)
To line up, line up, line up.	(point to the door or line up area, using your index finger as a 'bouncing ball' to show the action of lining up)
It's time to say 'goodbye'!	(point to your watch and wave)
Goodbye! Goodbye! Goodbye!	(wave)
Goodbye! Goodbye! Goodbye!	(wave)

3 Continue the chant as children collect their belongings and line up.
4 Finally, exchange goodbyes with each child as they leave the class.

Variation

Change the words to suit your 'goodbye' routine, for example,

It's time, it's time, it's time,
To get your bags and coats.
or
It's time, it's time, it's time,
To sit down, sit down, sit down
And wait for Mum and Dad.

Note

Photocopy the flashcard on the next page, write the words of the chant on the back and laminate it. Hold up the flashcard to signal this stage in the lesson. Read the words from the back of the flashcard instead of reading from the book.

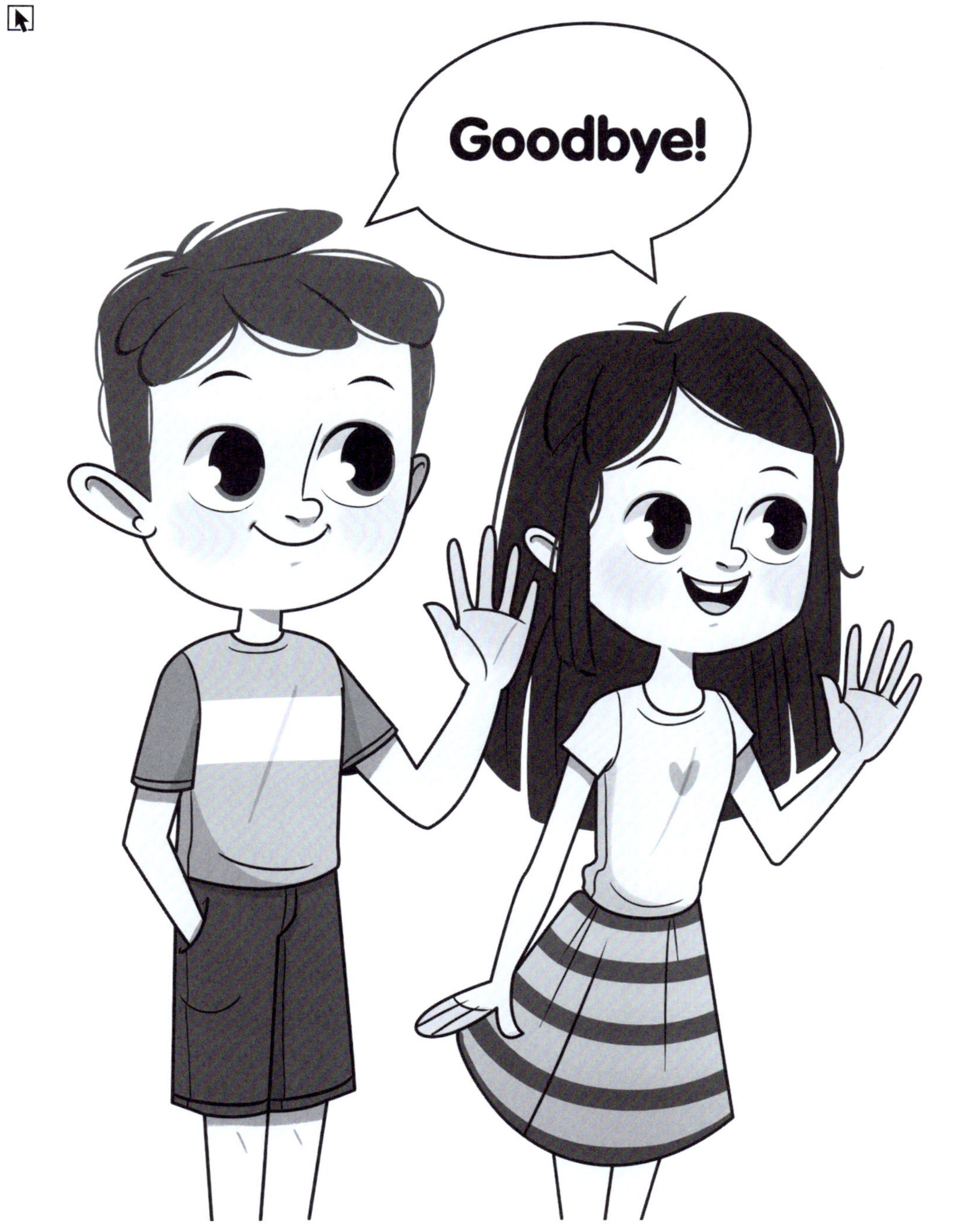
Goodbye!

2 Movement and games

Young children have a lot of energy. Integrating movement into your language activities is one of the great joys of teaching young learners, and it is also a very natural and direct way of making language meaningful. If the teacher says something and models it through movement – a gesture or a mime – children will often be able to make sense of the language intuitively. Children love imitating, so try to make your movements simple enough for them to copy. In this way they will enjoy making sense of the language and store it better in their memory.

Using games as one of our tools to transmit new language and make it familiar means that learning is fun and enjoyable. When children play, they are emotionally engaged and multiple sensory channels are activated in their brains (a game can involve looking, listening and moving all at the same time). This emotional and sensory involvement makes language all the more memorable.

The types of activities in this chapter vary from 'see, listen and do' games to those which require visual cues or special materials. Some are played in teams and others as a whole class, but all have simple rules. By learning to play according to rules, children practise important social behaviour, such as being part of a group. Very young learners don't usually enjoy competitive games; after all, they are only just learning to work together. For children to develop proper social skills, learning to cooperate is more important than winning. Once children reach primary school age, they like a little bit of competition, but the objective in the classroom should still be playing well rather than winning. Rather than giving a prize, reward winners with a cheer and a round of applause.

2.1 The countdown

Outline	Children do a countdown and pretend to be rockets lifting off.
Focus	Numbers 1–10, *What's the next number? What's the number before? rocket, countdown*
Age	5–7
Time	5–15 minutes
Materials	Optional: A picture of a rocket lifting off.
Preparation	None

Procedure

1 Count with the class from one to ten. Then say a number, e.g. *four*, and ask *What's the next number?* Use gesture (for example, pointing upwards) to help. Repeat with different numbers.

2 Say another number, e.g. *five*, and ask *What's the number before?* Use gesture to help again (for example, pointing downwards). Repeat with different numbers.

3 Show the children a picture of a rocket or draw one on the board.
Say *We are rockets, and we are going to fly into space. Let's do a countdown.* Count from ten to one in the style of a real countdown at a rocket launch. Do the same in the children's own language, if necessary.

4 Stand in a circle with the children. Say *Stretch!* and show them how to stretch up tall with their arms up. Start counting down (*Ten ... nine ... eight ...*) and with each number make yourself a bit smaller. When you get to *one*, crouch down very low, and then as you say *Zero!* jump up in the air.

5 Repeat the countdown, this time encouraging the children to copy the actions.

6 Practise the countdown and actions together. The children will start counting along with you.

Variations

1 Very young children can count from six to zero. Older children can start the countdown at 20.

2 Once the class are familiar with the activity, choose a confident child to lead the countdown.

2.2 Open the door

Outline	Children listen to a series of instructions and carry them out.
Focus	*Listen. It's the doorbell. Open the door. It's your friend. Say 'hello' and smile.*
Age	3–7
Time	10–15 minutes
Materials	Optional: Four pictures of the instructions (see page 56), coloured crayons for each child.
Preparation	None

Procedure

1 Stand in a circle with the children. Say *Listen*. Cup your ear with one hand. Make the sound of a doorbell and say *It's the doorbell*. Repeat this several times. Encourage the children to do the action and make the sound with you.

2 Say *Open the door*. Mime opening a door. Repeat this several times. Encourage the children to do the action with you.

3 Say all three sentences and do the actions again. Repeat several times. You will notice that the children will do the actions with you.

4 Add a new sentence *It's your friend*. Hold out both hands as if towards a friend. Repeat several times and encourage the children to do the action with you. Then start again from the top, with the children joining in.

5 Finally, add the sentence *Say 'hello' and smile*. Wave with one hand, then smile and trace the shape of a smiling mouth on your face with your finger. Repeat this several times, with the children.

6 When the children are very familiar with the mimes, say all the sentences – this time only the children do the actions:

> *Listen. It's the doorbell.*
> *Open the door.*
> *It's your friend.*
> *Say 'hello' and smile.*

7 Use gestures to show the children if they are right or wrong, e.g. nod your head to show the right action or point at a child who is doing the correct thing.

8 Once children can do the actions for the sentences in order, start mixing them up. Say, e.g. *Open the door*, and wait for the children to do the action.

Extension ideas

• Give the children pictures showing the four actions (see the next page or the website). Say the sentences in order and ask children to point to the correct picture. Then say the sentences in a jumbled order and get them to point again. Finally, ask children to listen and colour the circle next to each picture in the correct colour. Say, e.g. *Green – It's your friend. Red – Listen. It's the doorbell. Yellow – Say 'hello' and smile. Blue – Open the door.*

• Give the children variations of the instructions using language they already know, e.g. if they know *cat*, challenge them by saying *Listen. It's a cat*, then wait for a child to do the action and make a cat sound (not a doorbell). Other examples: *Listen. It's a car. / Listen. It's a plane. / Look. It's a dog.*

- When the children can say the instructions themselves they can work in pairs, taking turns to give instructions while their partner does the actions.

2.3 Talk like a robot

Outline	Children listen to instructions and carry them out, pretending to be robots.
Focus	Instructions, e.g. *Walk / Dance / Drive a car, … like a robot.*
Age	4–7
Time	5–15 minutes
Materials	None
Preparation	None

Procedure

1   In a computer-like, flat voice say *We're all robots now. Hello, robots! It's good to see you.*
2   Carry on talking in this way, encouraging the children to copy you. Then point to the children in front of you and say (still in your 'robot' voice) *Robots, can you say something?* Give the children a bit of time and wait for them to make an attempt at talking like a robot. When a child has said something, praise them, and repeat what they have said, modelling the robot voice. Get the whole class to repeat it.
3   Give instructions, and do robot-like actions or mimes for the children to copy, for example:

> *Walk like a robot.*
> *Dance like a robot.*
> *Write on the board like a robot.*
> *Make a phone call like a robot.*
> *Play football like a robot.*
> *Drive a car like a robot.*
> *Drink a glass of juice like a robot.*
> *Eat an ice cream like a robot.*

Variations

1   For older children, add *slowly / fast* to the instructions to make the game more challenging (e.g. *Walk slowly like a robot. Eat an ice cream quickly like a robot.*).
2   Play robot 'Simon says': the children only follow your instructions if you include *robot* (e.g. *Jump like a robot*). If you say, for example, *Point to the window*, the children who do the action (by mistake) need to sit down on the floor and miss a turn.
3   Use the question form *Can you …?* instead of direct instructions, e.g. *Can you play football like a robot? Can you say 'hello' like a robot?*

2.4 Opposites actions

Outline	Children do actions to learn opposites.
Focus	*yes, no, stop, go, open, close, hot, cold, big, small, short, tall, happy, sad, good, bad, up, down, turn around*
Age	4–7
Time	5–10 minutes
Materials	None
Preparation	Listen to the chant on the website.

Procedure

1 Stand in a circle with the children. Say the chant below and do the actions (in brackets) while children watch.

> *Yes* (nod) ... *No* (shake your head)
>
> *Stop* (make a 'stop' gesture with your hand) ... *Go* (walk on the spot)
>
> *Open* (open your hands as if opening a book) ... *Close* (close your hands as if closing a book)
>
> *Hot* (fan your face) ... *Cold* (shiver)
>
> *Big* (put your hands out wide) ... *Small* (make a ball with your hands)
>
> *Short* (put your hands beside your body with palms down) ... *Tall* (stretch your arms up)
>
> *Happy* (smile) ... *Sad* (frown)
>
> *Good* (thumbs up) ... *Bad* (thumbs down)
>
> *Up* (point up) ... *Down* (point down)
>
> *Turn around!* (turn around on the spot)

2 Say *Listen and do the actions*. Repeat the chant and the actions, with the children copying the actions.

3 Practise until the children join in with the words as well.

Variations

1 Once children know the actions, say the pairs of opposites in a different order. Children try to remember the correct action. It can be fun to do this really fast!

2 Children take turns to lead the activity.

3 Use a shorter version of the chant with younger children to practise fewer opposites (e.g. *Yes ... No, Stop ... Go, Happy ... Sad, Good ... Bad, Up ... Down, Turn around!*).

4 Add more pairs of opposites, with appropriate actions, for older children (rhyming words in brackets): *young, old (hot, cold), fast, slow (stop, go), stand up, sit down (smile, frown), black, white (day, night), find, lose (hat, shoes), walk, run (rain, sun), sit, stand (foot, hand)*.

2.5 The conga line action game

Outline	Children follow instructions and actions in a line.
Focus	Instructions, e.g. *Let's dance / play the guitar / point to the door / drive a car!*
Age	4–7
Time	3–5 minutes
Materials	None
Preparation	None

Procedure

1 Ask the children to line up, one behind the other, with you at the front of the line. Culture permitting, get the children to put their hands on the hips or shoulders of the person in front of them, making a conga line.

2 Walk around the classroom giving instructions. The children follow you and do the actions (in brackets) as they walk, for example:

Let's dance!	(dance)
Let's play the guitar!	(mime playing the guitar)
Let's point to the door!	(point in the direction of the classroom door)
Let's drive a car!	(mime turning a steering wheel)
Let's say 'hello'!	(wave)
Let's eat ice cream!	(mime licking an ice cream cone)

3 End the activity with *Let's sit down* (children sit down at their tables).

Variations

1 Repeat the same instructions until children know them by heart. Then children can take turns leading the conga line (giving the instructions themselves). Some children will no doubt add their own instructions – so much the better!

2 Additional instructions to try: *Let's run / jump / hop / sing / clap / stand up / put our hands up / put our hands down. Let's point to a table / window / chair / the clock / a child / the teacher. Let's play the piano / the drums / football / tennis / basketball / a computer game. Let's ride a bike / horse. Let's drive a van / bus. Let's fly a plane / kite. Let's eat a sandwich / an apple / a cake / pizza. Let's drink water. Let's talk on the telephone.*

Note

With large classes it is a good idea to play this game in the playground.

2.6 What number have I got?

Outline	Children guess the numbers on hidden flashcards.
Focus	Numbers 1–10, *What number is it? What number have I got? What's the last number? That's not the number. That's right. It's number (six).*
Age	4–6
Time	5–10 minutes
Materials	Number flashcards (1–10) or picture flashcards of words you want to practise (see *Variations*).
Preparation	None

Procedure

1 Write the numbers one to ten on the board in random order. As you write each number, ask *What number is it?* Practise the numbers with the class.

2 Hold a number flashcard so that the class can't see it. Ask individual children, e.g. *Sara, what number have I got?* The child guesses, e.g. *Six.* Say *That's not the number!* and ask a different child, e.g. *Jorge, what number have I got? …*

3 When a child guesses correctly, they come to the front and put a tick next to the number on the board. Show the number flashcard you were holding to confirm the answer and say *That's right. It's number (six).*

4 The child who guessed then chooses the next number flashcard and hides it while the rest of the class guess the number.

5 When there is just one flashcard left, ask *What's the last number?* Children guess as a class.

Variations

1 You can play this game with picture flashcards to practise vocabulary sets (as long as you can draw the items on the board). Go through the picture flashcards as a class first, so children know what the possibilities are, then draw pictures of the same items on the board. Follow the procedure from Step 2 above, holding one of the picture flashcards so that the class can't see it. Change the question you ask to match the type of words you practise. If you choose weather words (*sunny, cloudy, rainy, stormy, snowy*), for example, ask *What's the weather like?* If you decide to practise words for unrelated items (e.g. *book, cat, fish, sun, bus*), you can ask *What have I got?*

2 Play the Variation above with two identical sets of picture flashcards, if you prefer not to draw. Stick one set of flashcards on the board instead of drawing pictures. Use the other set for the guessing part of the game.

3 Instead of holding the flashcard which children have to guess in your hand or behind your back, put it in a box. The 'guessing box' adds an extra element of intrigue to the game.

2.7 Number line-up

Outline	Children hold number flashcards and line up in order.
Focus	Numbers 1–10, *Who's got number (one)? What number is it?*
Age	4–7
Time	5 minutes
Materials	Number flashcards (1–10) Optional: A card for each child and a marker pen.
Preparation	Make sure you have enough number flashcards to give one to each child. If you have a large class you will need more than one set.

Procedure

1 Show the number flashcards in order. Ask *What number is it?* Practise the numbers with the class.
2 Ask children to line up one behind the other (in two or three lines, if you have a large class).
3 Shuffle the number flashcards and give one to each child. Tell them not to show it to anyone else.
4 Ask *Who's got number one?* The child with this flashcard moves to the front of the line. Continue in this way, asking *Who's got number two?* etc. Encourage children to count with you while they line up.
5 When the children are lined up in order, ask each one to say their number (either from the front of the line to the back, or the back to the front).
6 Collect the flashcards quickly and repeat the game. Ask the children to move faster this time.

Variations

1 Ask children to line up with the largest number at the front (start with *Who's got number ten?*) so that they learn to count in both directions!
2 If you have a large class, play this as a team game with two sets of number flashcards. Line the children up in teams and give out the shuffled cards (the same numbers to each team). The team that lines up in order first is the winner. Make sure the teams speak as much English as they can while they play the game.

Note

Use this game to arrange the children in a line or a circle ready for a new activity.

2.8 Speed seeing

Outline	Children guess what number you are hiding behind your back.
Focus	Numbers 1–10, *What number is it?*
Age	4–6
Time	5 minutes
Materials	Optional: Number flashcards (1-10), letter cards or picture flashcards of words you want to practise (see *Variations*).
Preparation	None

Procedure

1 Ask the children to sit facing you. Place your hands behind your back, holding a number of fingers flat against your back, for example, seven. Tuck the other fingers in the palm of your hand.

2 Ask *What number can you see?* Turn around so that the children see your back (and the number of fingers you are showing) for a second or less.

3 Face the children again and ask *What number is it?*

4 Children tell you the number of fingers they saw. They can either say their answers in open class or, if you want this to be a quiet game, choose a child to say the number each time.

Variations

1 You can play the game without turning around. Just hold up a number of fingers in front of the class for a couple of seconds, instead of behind your back.

2 Use number flashcards instead of holding your fingers against your back. Hold the flashcard so it faces the children when you turn around.

3 Play the game with letter cards, colour flashcards or pictures of other known animals or objects (show the card for a second and ask *What can you see?*).

4 With older children who can recognize words, play the game with word cards.

Note

This game is especially fun to play if you have a few minutes at the end of the lesson, when it's acceptable for the whole class to shout out their answers!

2.9 What's missing?

Outline	Children say which object is missing from a set.
Focus	Topic vocabulary, e.g. numbers, classroom objects, animals, transport or a mixture of learned words, *What's missing? Close / Open your eyes.*
Age	4–6
Time	5–10 minutes
Materials	Optional: Set of flashcards from one topic / various flashcards, sticky tack.
Preparation	Optional: Make a set of six to ten mini flashcards for each small group (see *Extension ideas*).

Procedure

1 Write five or so numbers on the board randomly (for example, 6, 2, 5, 3, 1).
2 Point to each number and ask *What number is it?* Children say the number.
3 Tell the children to close their eyes. Erase a number from the board.
4 The children open their eyes. Ask *What's missing?* The children guess.

Variations

1 Draw pictures instead of writing numbers. Point to each picture and ask *What's this?* Children say the words. Erase a picture when the children close their eyes and ask *What's missing?* as above.
2 Use picture flashcards rather than drawing or writing. Remove a flashcard from the board when the children close their eyes. You can use the same flashcards and move them around on the board, taking a different flashcard down each time.
3 At step 3 of the Procedure, ask a child to come up and erase a picture / number or take a flashcard away, while the rest of the class close their eyes.

Extension ideas

• Once children are familiar with the game, they can play it in pairs or small groups. Give each pair / group a set of mini flashcards (or number cards). They put all the flashcards face up on the table. The children turn around or close their eyes while one child in the group takes away a flashcard. Then they look again and guess. The child who guesses the missing flashcard takes a turn.
• Play *Odd one out* with flashcards. Place a group of four flashcards (with an 'odd one out') on the board. Point to each flashcard and ask *What's this?* Children say, e.g. *cat, dog, book, fish.* Ask *Which one is different?* Children guess (e.g. the book). Older children or those who are familiar with *Odd one out* can take turns choosing the four flashcards (with their own 'odd one out') for the class to guess.

2.10 What's in the bag?

Outline	Children guess objects which are hidden in a bag.
Focus	*What is it? Is it a…? bag*, names of different objects (e.g. *egg, house, bear, car, apple, pencil*)
Age	4–7
Time	5 minutes
Materials	A bag and six objects / toys made from different materials (e.g. toy vehicles, classroom objects, plastic food, soft toy animals). Although children do not have to have seen the objects in the bag before, they need to know what they are called in English.
Preparation	Put the six items (for example, a plastic egg, a wooden house, a soft toy bear, a metal car, a plastic apple, a pencil) into a bag.

Procedure

1   Hold up the bag with items inside and say *Look at my bag*. Shake the bag and ask *What's in it?* Close your eyes and take something out of the bag. Feel the object for a while, still with your eyes closed, showing that you're thinking. Ask, e.g. *Is it a bear?* The class says *Yes!* Say *Now it's your turn*.

2   Choose a child who's sitting quietly and attentively. Say *Close your eyes. Take one thing from the bag. … What is it?* The child closes their eyes, takes an object and holds it so the class can see it. Then they feel it (still with eyes closed), guessing what it is (e.g. *Car?*). The rest of the class say *Yes* or *No*. When the child has guessed correctly, put the object on the table and choose the next child to play.

3   Finish the activity when the bag is empty. Assure children that others will have a go next lesson.

2.11 Animal mimes

Outline	Children guess the animals you mime.
Focus	*What animal is this / am I?* animals (e.g. *dog, cat, butterfly, snake, elephant*)
Age	4–6
Time	5–10 minutes
Materials	Six to ten animal flashcards.
Preparation	None

Procedure

1 Show the animal flashcards one by one and ask *What animal is this?* Say, e.g. *That's right, it's an elephant.* and stick each flashcard on the board.

2 Mime one of the animals, for example, lift your arm in front of your face to make the trunk of an elephant. Ask *What animal am I?* The children guess, e.g. *You're an elephant!* or *Elephant!* Say *That's right! Elephant!* The whole class repeats the animal word.

3 Once children have learned the animal mimes, they can take turns choosing to be an animal for the rest of the class to guess.

Variations

1 Once children are familiar with the animal mimes, use this as a group movement activity. All the children in the class line up, one behind the other. Stand at the head of the line and move around the classroom miming an animal and saying, e.g. *Be a cat!* Children follow you in a conga line and do the appropriate mime. Change the instruction, e.g. *Now be an elephant.* The children change their mime.

2 Play a form of *Simon Says*. The children do an animal mime only if you say *Teacher says* (e.g. *Teacher says* 'Be *an elephant*.'). Children who mime when you don't say *Teacher says* – or who do the wrong mime – are 'out'. They watch the rest of the group and help you to decide who else is 'out'. Continue until there's a winner. Alternatively, children only do an animal mime if you say *please* (e.g. *Be an elephant, please*).

3 Put all the animal flashcards in a box. Take out a flashcard but don't show the class. Do the mime for the animal on the flashcard. The children guess. Whoever guesses the animal correctly takes the next animal flashcard out of the box and mimes.

💡 **Tip**

The game can be used to revise any other groups of words which are easy to mime (e.g. forms of transport (mime driving / riding on transport), classroom objects (mime using the objects), clothes (mime putting on the clothes)).

2.12 Question and answer basketball

Outline	Children play a team game. They practise answering questions, earning extra points by throwing a ball into a basketball net.
Focus	Questions, e.g. *What's this? How old are you? What's the weather like today?*
Age	6–7
Time	10–15 minutes
Materials	A soft ball and a toy basketball net (or a scrunched up piece of paper and an empty container, such as a wastepaper bin). Small pieces of card for questions. You will need eight to ten questions.
Preparation	Write a set of questions which children have practised on pieces of card (see *Procedure* for examples). Attach the basketball net to the wall at a reasonable height for small players. If possible, mark a line on the floor so that children know where to stand to throw the ball.

Procedure

1 Divide the class into two teams. The teams line up facing the basketball net. Give the soft ball to the first child in the team having the first turn.

2 Read out a question from one of your cards, e.g. *What's your name?* If the child answers the question correctly, they get a point for the team. Then they can try to score a second point by throwing the ball through the basketball net. Then the first child in the other team has a turn. Keep score on the board.

3 Good questions to use include *What's this* (point to an object or picture in the classroom)? *How old are you? What's the weather like today? What colour is the car / star / table / chair* (point to it in a picture or in the classroom)? *Do you like ice cream / pizza / apples / fish? How many girls / boys are there today? What's his / her name? Can you jump / sing / hop / drive a car / ride a bike?* (the child needs to do an action to show the answer to questions with 'can').

4 Play the game until each child has had two or three turns, then count the scores to declare a winning team.

Variation

Instead of asking questions, show flashcards of familiar objects. The child gets a point for saying the word and then another if they throw the ball through the net. This works best if it's played quickly, with lots of flashcards from different vocabulary sets.

> 💡 **Tip**
>
> Very young children often don't understand or enjoy competitive team games. You could use this game for number practice instead. Children take turns to try and throw the ball into a bin or other container (very young children find this easier than throwing into a hoop). The class counts aloud together. The game ends when they reach ten.

2.13 Flyswatter fun

Outline	Children play a team game. They slap flashcards on a wall with a flyswatter to win points.
Focus	Vocabulary sets, e.g. food (*apple, banana, strawberry, chicken, sandwich, ice cream, hamburger, water, milk*)
Age	5–7
Time	5–10 minutes
Materials	Two plastic flyswatters or rolled-up papers, a set of flashcards, sticky tack. You can play the game without flyswatters (children use their hands) but flyswatters make it more exciting. Optional: A set of word cards with the same vocabulary as the flashcards (see *Variation* 3).
Preparation	Stick the picture flashcards on a wall or on the board at a height children can reach. If possible, draw a line on the floor so that children know where to stand to play (at least a metre away from the board).

Procedure

1   Ask children to name the objects on the flashcards.
2   Divide the class into two teams. The teams line up facing the flashcards. Give the first child in each team a flyswatter.
3   Choose one of the items on the wall and say, e.g. *It's an apple!* The two children at the front of the teams run and try to slap the correct picture flashcard with their flyswatters. The first child to slap the correct flashcard wins a point for their team. The children then go to the back of the line and the two children at the front of each team have their turn. Keep score on the board.
4   Continue in this way. Ask children in the line to choose the next item on the wall and say it. This ensures that the children waiting for their turn are still interested in the game.
5   Play until each child has had two or three turns, then count the scores and declare a winning team.

Variations

1   If you prefer to play the game in a calmer way, say a word for each child (so they are not both trying to hit the same flashcard). Whoever slaps their flashcard first gets a point for their team.
2   Say four of the items instead of one. The child with the flyswatter has to slap the four flashcards you say in the correct order. Once they are familiar with this version of the game, the children take turns saying four items, while one of their classmates slaps the flashcards with the flyswatter in the correct order.
3   Play the game with a set of word cards to match the picture flashcards. Instead of saying an item, hold up the word card. The children at the front of the teams read the word and try to slap the matching flashcard on the wall.

3 Songs, chants and rhymes for topics

Songs, chants and rhymes are of fundamental importance in the early learner classroom. Having fun is a key element of learning, and lively tunes and rhymes motivate children to participate in a way that is natural for them. Repeating songs, chants and rhymes is also an ideal way to help children get the rhythm of English right. English is a stress-timed language, which means that stressed syllables are spoken at fairly regular intervals, and unstressed syllables often become shorter or disappear completely. But if the children's own language is syllable-timed, they will be used to giving each syllable the same amount of stress when they speak.

Songs, chants and rhymes also have a positive effect on memory. The more catchy and inspiring they are, the better children will remember the language. They will remember not just single words, but also, and maybe more importantly, whole strings of words. These groups of words that are stored as whole units in the brain are called 'lexical chunks'. If children learn to say, e.g. *Let's play firefighters*, and the teacher gives them lots of opportunities to practise this chunk and use it in various contexts, then they will remember *Let's play …* as an item, and not as a collection of individual words. They will find it easier to use the phrase when they want to say, for example, *Let's play a game*.

Besides those we have provided, remember that you can often change the words to songs, chants or rhymes. For example, altering the words to 'The conga monster chant' (activity 3.4) is a great way to create versions to suit your children's age, language level and the topic of your lesson. Have fun with the chants and rhymes and involve your young learners even more by encouraging them to say the words in different ways: loudly, whispering, in a deep or silly voice, like a monster, etc. See the *Activities for Very Young Learners* website for recordings and extra material to accompany some of the activities found in this chapter. This material is indicated with the symbol [▶].

69

3.1 The classroom chant

Outline	Children say a chant and point to objects around the classroom.
Focus	*Point to the …, window, door, board, floor, table, pen, chair, Start again! That's the end!*
Age	3–7
Time	2–5 minutes
Materials	None
Preparation	Listen to the chant on the website.

Procedure

1 Say the chant, pointing to the things in the classroom as you go along:

Point to the window,
Point to the door,
Point to the board,
Point to the floor.

Point to a table,
Point to a pen,
Point to a chair,
And start again!

2 Repeat the chant several times. Younger children join in with the actions. Older children can join in with the actions and words.

3 When you want to stop, change the last line to *And that's the end!*

Variations

1 Once children are familiar with the chant, say it faster and faster to make it more challenging.

2 Vary the words of the chant by using *Point to …* and other things the children can see in the classroom, for example, colours and shapes.

3 Play a lip-reading game, mouthing the instructions from the chant in random order, e.g. *Point to a chair*. Children watch your lips and point to the object.

3.2 Ten little bugs

Outline	Children sing a numbers song about bugs.
Focus	Numbers 1–10, *How many bugs? little, sitting, chair, into the air, there are*
Age	5–7 (for three and four year-olds, see *Variation 1*, below)
Time	2–5 minutes
Materials	You can either use your fingers to represent the bugs or ten plastic insects / 'bugs' made from buttons or other small objects. Optional: Wooden buttons, paper and glue for children to make their own bugs (see *Extension ideas*).
Preparation	Listen to the song on the website or sing it to the tune of *Ten Green Bottles*.

Procedure

1 Place your ten fingertips (or ten bugs) on a chair. Sing the first four lines of the song to the tune of *Ten green bottles*:

> *Ten little bugs,*
> *Sitting on a chair!*
> *Ten little bugs,*
> *Sitting on a chair!*

2 Lift one hand and show your index finger 'flying away' (or take one of the bugs off the chair) and sing:

> *One little bug flies into the air …*

Then put nine fingertips on the chair and sing the last two lines of the song:

> *And there are nine little bugs,*
> *Sitting on the chair.*

3 Sing the song again, but this time starting with *Nine little bugs* … Repeat the song, taking away a bug each time, until there are no little bugs left on the chair. The last line is:

> *And there are no little bugs, sitting on the chair!*

4 Once children have learned the song, the whole class sing and do the actions with you.

Variations

1 With three and four year-olds, start the song with *Five little bugs* … Make a chair with your left hand by having your palm facing upwards and your fingers held together at a right angle to your palm. Place the five fingertips of your right hand on the palm of your left hand.

2 Draw a large chair with ten bugs on it on the board. Instead of using your fingers to represent the bugs in the song, erase a bug from the board each time a bug 'flies away' while you sing. Once the children are familiar with the song, choose a volunteer to come to the front and erase the bugs.

Extension ideas
- Choose ten different children to stand at the front and act as the bugs. Each time a bug 'flies into the air' in the song, one of the children mimes flying away and goes back to their seat.
- Children make their own bugs by gluing paper wings to wooden buttons with white glue. The children place the ten bugs on their chairs, and remove them one by one as they sing the song.
- Show photographs of different kinds of bugs, e.g. ladybirds, beetles, spiders, mosquitoes, flies and bees. Talk about the differences between them, e.g. number of legs, if they fly, what they eat.

3.3 The shapes pointing song

Outline	Children find shapes around the room while you sing a song.
Focus	Shapes, e.g. *circle, square, triangle, rectangle, star; Point to a (square). Can you see a (circle)? Now point to it, please.*
Age	4–6
Time	5–10 minutes
Materials	Optional: Shape flashcards in different colours (see *Variation*).
Preparation	Listen to the song on the website or sing it to the tune of *Did you ever see a lassie?*

Procedure

1 Revise shapes by showing examples in the classroom (e.g. point to the board and say *It's a rectangle.*). Then ask the children to stand up and point to different shapes around the room: *Point to a (square).* It's quite amazing how many objects in the room are made up of shapes. The children will find some that you haven't seen!

2 Sing the song below to the tune of *Did you ever see a lassie?* Make the different shapes with your fingers as you sing the questions:

> *Can you see a circle, a circle, a circle?*
> *Can you see a circle? Now point to it, please!*
>
> *Can you see a square, a square, a square?*
> *Can you see a square? Now point to it, please!*

3 Continue the song, adding more shapes, if you wish, e.g. *triangle, rectangle, oval, star.*

Variation

Stick flashcards of shapes in different colours on the walls. Add colours to the song, e.g. *Can you see a red circle …?* The children point to the flashcards rather than objects in the room.

Extension idea

Make the magic wands from Activity 5.1 (page 116). As you sing the song, children use the wands to point to the different shapes.

3.4 The conga monster chant

Outline	Children form a 'monster' by standing in a line and practise classroom items.
Focus	Classroom items (or other vocabulary sets)
Age	3–7
Time	5 minutes
Materials	None
Preparation	Listen to the chant on the website.

Procedure

1 Ask the children to line up, one behind the other, with you at the front of the line. Culture permitting, get the children to put their hands on the hips or shoulders of the person in front of them, making a conga line.

2 Tiptoe forward (with the children following) and quietly say *I'm a monster. A monster.*

3 Stop walking. Rub your belly with one hand indicating that the 'monster' is hungry, and say, this time more loudly *I'm hungry. I'm hungry.*

4 Look around, as if for food, and say, quietly again *What can I eat? What can I eat?*

5 Pause for a moment, then point at an object that children know the word for, and quietly say, e.g. *The table. The table.*

6 Tiptoe over to the object (with the children following). Mime eating greedily like a monster and say quite loudly

> *Yummy, yummy, yummy!*
> *Munch, munch, munch!*
> *The table. The table.*
> *Yummy, yummy, yummy!*
> *Munch, munch, munch!*

7 Repeat the chant over several lessons, so that the children get really familiar with the language. Gradually, make the 'monster' eat different objects in the classroom (always ones the children already know in English, e.g. *door, chair, board, books, pencils*).

Variations

1 Once the children are familiar with the chant, invite a confident child to take over the first position in the conga line and be the monster.

2 Use the chant to practise different vocabulary sets, e.g. fruit, clothes or parts of the body. The 'monster' pretends to eat either real objects or flashcards / pictures of the items on the walls.

3.5 It's cold outside

Outline	Children sing a song about the weather with actions.
Focus	Weather: *sunny, cold, rainy, windy, snowy, stormy*; Clothes: *T-shirt, umbrella, hat, scarf; I look out of the window, What do I see? It's (cold) outside. put on, get, say 'goodbye', sit on the sofa*
Age	4–7
Time	5 minutes
Materials	Weather flashcards or photographs of different kinds of weather, a T-shirt, umbrella, hat and scarf.
Preparation	Listen to the song on the website.

Procedure

1 Use weather flashcards or photographs to practise weather conditions. Show each picture and ask *What's the weather like?* Children reply, e.g. *It's sunny.*

2 Present or revise *T-shirt, umbrella, hat* and *scarf* using real items or by drawing pictures.

3 Sing the song below and do the actions in brackets (the actions for repeated lines are the same):

I look out of the window,	(make a square with your fingers and then look out of it)
And what do I see?	(mime looking)
It's sunny!	(speak this line, rather than singing)
I put on a T-shirt …	(mime putting on a T-shirt)
And say 'goodbye'!	(wave, mime opening a door and stepping outside)
Oh no!	
It's cold outside!	(shiver and then mime opening the door and going back inside)
I look out of the window,	
And what do I see?	
It's rainy!	
I get my umbrella …	(mime fetching an umbrella)
And say 'goodbye'!	
Oh no!	
It's windy outside!	(mime the wind blowing you and your umbrella away, then mime opening the door and going back inside)
I look out of the window,	
And what do I see?	
It's snowy!	
I put on a hat and scarf …	(mime putting on a hat and a scarf)
And say 'goodbye'!	
Oh no!	
It's stormy outside!	(look up at the sky as if frightened, then mime opening the door and going back inside)

> *I look out of the window,*
> *And what do I see?*
> *It's stormy!*
> *I sit on the sofa…* (sit down, as if on a sofa)
> *And say, 'What a fantastic storm!'* (thumbs up)

Variation

When you get to the line 'And what do I see?' let the children decide what the weather is like in the next part of the song. Ask, e.g. *And what do I see, Ahmed?* Ahmed replies *It's cloudy!*

Extension ideas

- If you have an interactive whiteboard, you could make slides showing sunny, rainy, snowy and stormy weather through a window, interspersed with different weather conditions outside. Sing the song, with children calling out the weather they see on the slide, both through the window and outside.
- Talk about how the weather changes and extreme weather.

Notes

- This song is very simple to sing. It is in the style of a marching song and the middle and last line of every verse is spoken rather than sung. Add this song to your weather routine during circle time or teach it when covering the topic of clothes.
- This song is inspired by one Karen learned from Rowan Hardman.

3.6 I can jump, I can hop

Outline	Children perform an action chant, changing one verb each time.
Focus	Verbs: *jump, hop, clap, run, dance, sit, stop; I can* ….
Age	3–5
Time	2 minutes
Materials	None
Preparation	Listen to the chant on the website.

Procedure

1 Children stand up facing you in a line, rows or a circle.

2 Say the following chant and do the actions (in brackets):

I can jump,	(jump)
I can hop,	(hop)
I can clap,	(clap your hands)
And I can stop!	(freeze like a statue)
I can jump,	(jump)
I can hop,	(hop)
I can run,	(run on the spot)
And I can stop!	(freeze like a statue)
I can jump,	(jump)
I can hop,	(hop)
I can dance,	(dance)
And I can stop!	(freeze like a statue)
I can jump,	(jump)
I can hop,	(hop)
I can sit,	(sit down)
And I can stop!	(freeze like a statue, sitting down)

Variations

1 Use different verbs (e.g. *walk, point, eat, drink, swim, fly, get dressed, sing, cook, drive, ski*).

2 Make a conga line (see page 59, Procedure step 1) and do the chant. This variation is useful if you want to move to a different part of the classroom for the next activity.

3 Older children can suggest ideas for the last action in each verse.

Extension idea

Use verb phrases, e.g. *ride a bike, play football / the guitar, make a cake, be happy / angry / a tiger*.

Note

This is a great 'wake up' chant if your class is getting restless. It is useful when first learning actions. The fun comes not only from miming, but from freezing like a statue when everyone says *And I can stop!*

3.7 Happy animals

Outline	Children sing about animals and mime the things they do.
Focus	Animals: *monkey, penguin, giraffe, frog*, etc; *Can you…?* Actions (passive understanding only): *swing, waddle, munch, hop*, etc.
Age	3–7
Time	5 minutes
Materials	None
Preparation	Listen to the song on the website.

Procedure

1 Sing the following song and do the actions (in brackets). Everyone sings the verses but just the teacher says the lines marked 'Teacher'.

I'm a happy, happy monkey,
And this is what I do,
I swing, swing, swing,   (mime swinging from branch to branch)
Can you swing too?

Teacher: *Swing everyone!*

I'm a happy, happy penguin,
And this is what I do,
I waddle, waddle, waddle,   (mime waddling like a penguin)
Can you waddle too?

Teacher: *Waddle everyone!*

I'm a happy, happy giraffe,
And this is what I do,
I munch, munch, munch,   (hold one arm up to make a giraffe's neck and use your thumb
                                        and fingers to make a mouth, opening and closing as if eating
                                        leaves)

Can you munch too?

Teacher: *Munch everyone!*

I'm a happy, happy frog,
And this is what I do,
I jump, jump, jump,   (crouch down on the floor and jump up)
Can you jump too?

Teacher: *Jump everyone!*

Variations

1 Use other animals and actions: *fish – swim* (mime swimming); *snake – slither* (put your palms together in front of you and move them forward in a slithering motion); *elephant – trumpet*

(hold one arm out in front of you and move it up and down like a trunk); *dog – wag* (put your arm behind your back and swing it like a tail); *cat – lick* (mime a cat cleaning its paw); *kangaroo – hop* (mime jumping like a kangaroo); *butterfly – flutter*; *bird – fly*.

2   Perform the words as a chant and change your voice for each animal.

Notes

- This song is a great way to transition between activities, to bring everyone back together or to wrap up a lesson. You can sing just one verse if you are moving the class from one place to another or perform as many verses as you like.
- If you want to use this as a calming activity or when the children are sitting, sing it more quietly and choose animals with mimes which can be done in a seated position (e.g. *monkey, giraffe, elephant, cat, bird*).

3.8 Have some chicken

Outline	Children perform a chant and learn how to offer food.
Focus	Food: *chicken, rice, carrots, peas, apples, pie, strawberries; Have some (chicken)!, lovely, Don't be shy.*
Age	4–6
Time	10–15 minutes
Materials	Flashcards or pictures of food: chicken, rice, carrots, peas, apples, pie, strawberries.
Preparation	Listen to the chant on the website.

Procedure

1 Teach *lovely* and *shy*, using mime to illustrate the meaning. You could teach the expression *Don't be shy* using the 'sandwiching' technique (see *Introduction*, page 13).

2 Present the chant by first saying it rhythmically all the way through. Then get the children to say the 'lovely' lines, as shown below.

Teacher:	*Have some chicken.*
Class:	*Lovely chicken!*
Teacher:	*Have some rice.*
Class:	*Lovely rice!*
Teacher:	*Have some carrots.*
Class:	*Lovely carrots!*
Teacher:	*Have some peas.*
Class:	*Lovely peas!*
Teacher:	*Have some apples.*
	Have some pie.
	Have some strawberries.
	Don't be shy.

Variations

1 When the children can say the chant really well, divide the class into two groups. One group says the *Have some…* lines and the other half says the *Lovely…* lines.

2 Teach younger children a shorter version of the chant – just the last four lines. They can all mime offering the food as they say the lines.

Extension idea

Get the class to sit at their tables. Ask two or three children to walk round pretending to carry trays full of imaginary food. They approach the children sitting at the tables and offer them some of the imaginary food, saying e.g. *(Ken), have some chicken.* Children who have been offered the food respond *Yes, lovely* or *No, thanks.*

Note

We learned this chant from Günter Gerngross, Herbert's co-author on *Super Safari* (Cambridge University Press, 2015).

3.9 I don't like chips

Outline	Children sing a song about food and likes / dislikes.
Focus	Food: *chips, carrots, sausages, apples, cakes, ice cream; I like (apples). I don't like (chips); yes, no*
Age	5–7
Time	15–20 minutes
Materials	Food flashcards or pictures of food: chips, carrots, sausages, apples, cakes, ice cream. Optional: A copy of the worksheet on page 82 for each child (see *Extension idea*).
Preparation	Listen to the song on the website. Download or copy the worksheet if you are doing the Extension activity.

Procedure

1   Say a food item or show a flashcard, e.g. sausages, and say *I like sausages. Yummy!* Use mime and gesture to show the meaning. Repeat with a different food item, e.g. carrots, and say *I don't like carrots. Yuk!* Practise *Yummy!* and *Yuk!* with the class.

2   Then say food words and / or show flashcards to different children. They say *Yummy!* if they like the food or *Yuk!* if they don't. Older children can also say *I like ….* or *I don't like …*

3   Teach the song, gradually encouraging the children to join in (by humming and then singing along).

> *I don't like chips – no, no, no.*
> *I don't like carrots – no, no, no.*
> *I don't like sausages – no, no, no.*
> *No, no, no, no, NO!*
>
> *Chips, Oh, no! Carrots, Oh no!*
> *Sausages – no, no, no, no, NO!*
>
> *I like apples – yes, yes, yes.*
> *I like cakes – yes, yes, yes.*
> *I like ice cream – yes, yes, yes.*
> *Yes, yes, yes, yes, YES!*
>
> *Apples, Oh, yes! Cakes, Oh yes!*
> *Ice cream – yes, yes, yes, yes, YES!*

Extension idea

•   Children complete the worksheet as they listen to the song (see page 82 or the website). You will find detailed instructions for this Extension idea on the website.

Note

The song and the worksheet come from *Super Safari Student's Book 3* (Cambridge University Press, 2015).

3.10 Look at my clown

Outline	Children perform a chant about the colour of clothes.
Focus	Clothes: *jeans, socks, shirt, glasses*; Colours: *green, yellow, pink, blue, red, orange*; *Look at my clown. Their name's … . Their (jeans) are (yellow)*, *parrot, zoo*
Age	5–6
Time	10–15 minutes
Materials	Real items of clothing (as listed above) or clothes flashcards, picture of a parrot. Two simple drawings of clowns, one male, one female with clothes coloured in according to the words of the chant below (there are pictures to copy on page 84). Optional: Sheets of paper and crayons.
Preparation	Draw the clowns, colour them in and display the pictures on the board or on the wall. Listen to the chant on the website.

Procedure

1 Say a clothes word from the chant (e.g. *socks*). The children point to a real item of clothing or the correct flashcard. Get them to repeat each word several times.

2 Show the picture of a parrot or draw one on the board. Teach the word. Teach / revise *zoo*.

3 Present the picture of the male clown. Say *Look, this is my clown. His name's Bozo.*

4 Say the first verse of the chant rhythmically, getting the children to repeat the lines as shown below:

Teacher:	*Look at my clown.*
Class:	*Look at my clown.*
Teacher:	*His jeans are green.*
Class:	*His jeans are green.*
Teacher:	*His socks are yellow.*
Class:	*His socks are yellow.*
Teacher:	*His glasses are pink.*
Class:	*His glasses are pink.*
Teacher:	*His shirt is blue.*
Class:	*His shirt is blue.*
All:	*Green and yellow*
	Pink and blue.
	Like a parrot
	In a zoo!

5 Present the picture of the female clown. Say *Look This is my clown. Her name's Pippa.*

6 Say the second verse of the chant line by line, as above:

Teacher:	*Look at my clown.*
Class:	*Look at my clown.*
Teacher:	*Her jeans are red.*
Class:	*Her jeans are red.*
Teacher:	*Her socks are orange.*
Class:	*Her socks are orange.*

Teacher:	*Her glasses are green.*
Class:	*Her glasses are green.*
Teacher:	*Her shirt is blue.*
Class:	*Her shirt is blue.*
All:	*Red and orange*
	Green and blue.
	Like a parrot
	In a zoo!

Variation

With younger children, teach just one verse of the chant, using just one clown picture.

Extension ideas

• When the children know the chant well, play a memory game that is also a fun drill of the possessive adjectives *his* and *her*. Give the children time to look at the pictures of the clowns and remember the colour of their clothes. Then put the pictures on your desk face down. Say an item of clothing from the chant, e.g. *socks*. The children respond by saying the correct lines (and remembering *His* or *Her* at the beginning), e.g. *His socks are yellow. Her socks are orange.* Show them the pictures and check the colours together.

• With older classes, get the children to draw their own clown and present it to the class, e.g. *This is my clown. Her name's … Her jeans are … Her socks are …*

Figure 3.1: Clown pictures to copy on the board and colour

3.11 The *Get dressed* chant

Outline	The children perform a chant and mime getting dressed.
Focus	*shorts, T-shirt, socks, trainers, tennis, football, basketball; Wake up (sleepy head), Get out of bed, Put on your (shorts). Let's play (tennis). Let's ride a bike.*
Age	4–6
Time	5–10 minutes
Materials	Optional: A paper doll with the clothes in the chant (see *Extension idea*).
Preparation	Listen to the chant on the website.

Procedure

1 Teach the chant below, with the actions (in brackets):

Wake up sleepy head,	(make a pillow with your palms, lift your head)
Get out of bed,	(mime getting up and stretching)
My mother said!	(put your hands on your hips)
Put on your shorts,	(mime putting on shorts)
Put on your T-shirt,	(mime putting on a T-shirt)
Put on your socks,	(mime putting on socks)
Put on your trainers!	(mime putting on trainers)
Let's play tennis,	(mime playing tennis)
My mother said!	(put your hands on your hips)

2 Repeat the chant three more times, but each time change the last two lines so they are about different sports: *Let's play football, Let's play basketball* and *Let's ride a bike*.

Variations

1 Use weather vocabulary and different clothes to change the topic of the chant: e.g.

Put on your hat,	*Put on your coat,*	*Put on your boots,*
Put on your sandals,	*Put on your gloves,*	*Put on your raincoat,*
It's sunny outside,	*It's cold outside,*	*It's rainy outside,*
My mother said!	*My mother said!*	*My mother said!*

2 Use different family words in the final line of each verse instead of *mother*, e.g. *father, sister, brother* or *the baby*.

Extension idea

Make paper dolls with cut-out paper T-shirts, shorts, socks and trainers. Children colour the doll and clothes and cut out the pictures. They dress the paper doll while they say the chant.

3.12 Let's play firefighters

Outline	The children sing a song about jobs and clothes.
Focus	*firefighter, teacher, Let's play (firefighters); I'm a (firefighter). How about you? My trousers are black. My hat is yellow. I've got a lot of pencils. I've got paper too.*
Age	5–6
Time	15–20 minutes
Materials	Flashcard or picture of a firefighter.
Preparation	Listen to the song on the website.

Procedure

1 Use the flashcard and mime to teach or revise *firefighter*.
2 Say *Let's play firefighters*. Shout *A fire. Look! Put on your black trousers. Put on your shoes. Put on your helmet. Get into the fire engine.* Mime getting dressed, climbing into the fire engine, putting on the seatbelt, etc. The children copy your actions. Say *Let's go!* Mime driving the fire engine, and get the children to join in with you. Then say, *OK. We're here. Let's get out. Let's fight the fire.* Mime fighting the fire and encourage the children to join in (with imaginary hoses).
3 Play the song. The children hum and then sing along.

> *Let's play firefighters.*
> *Let's play firefighters.*
> *I'm a firefighter …*
> *How about you?*
>
> *My trousers are black.*
> *My shoes are yellow.*
> *And my hat is yellow too.*
>
> *I'm a firefighter …*
> *How about you?*
>
> *Let's play teachers.*
> *Let's play teachers.*
> *I'm a teacher …*
> *How about you?*
>
> *I've got a lot of pencils.*
> *I've got paper too.*
> *I'm a teacher …*
> *How about you?*
>
> *I'm a teacher …*
> *How about you?*

Extension idea

When the children are familiar with the song, do a series of mimes for a different job, e.g. taxi driver, for the children to copy. Say *Let's play taxi drivers*. Mime driving a car. Shout *Taxi! Taxi!* Then mime noticing someone from the taxi and stopping the car. Say *Hello! Where do you want to go? To the train station? OK. Let's go!* Mime driving again. Say *Here we are! Ten pounds, please.* Mime taking the money and say *Thank you. Goodbye!* You could do similar mimes for *cook, farmer* and *scientist*.

Note

The song and the idea for the 'Let's play firefighters' game come from *Super Safari Student's Book 2* (Cambridge University Press, 2015).

4   Stories and storytelling

Stories are deeply rooted in the human experience. There was a time when we sat around a campfire listening to the stories of our tribe – stories that shaped our identity and destiny. Today we usually read a book or sit in front of a screen to get our fill of adventure and excitement, and of course, we also tell our own stories every day.

No wonder stories are such an important part of early years education. But storytelling is often more than educational. It is a special moment of connection between a child and an adult. When the classroom is filled with a shared excitement or concern, when everyone is quietly waiting for the next word or turn of the page, one truly feels the magic of being a teacher of very young children.

We can't always know which stories will capture our children's imagination and attention. They will not eagerly ask us to read every story again and again. However, there are some key factors which seem to make a story successful in the classroom. We can identify attractive characters, repetition of language or sound effects and a clear, interesting storyline as some features of children's favourite tales, but the manner of telling the story is also an essential factor for success.

When telling a traditional story (see 4.9 *The Enormous Turnip*), don't try to memorize it word for word. Remember the main points, practise the gestures you will need to use beforehand and then tell the story in your own words, encouraging the children to copy your actions and language. For more advice on storytelling see *Storytelling with picture books*, in 'Tips for teaching very young learners', (Tip 5, on page 23).

In this chapter you will find original and classic stories, each with a suggested procedure to make the story accessible to your young learners. Follow-up activities, including craft projects and display ideas are also provided.

4.1 Are you my mummy?

Outline	Children listen to a story about a chick who can't find her mother. They follow it with the help of pictures.
Focus	*I'm hungry. Where's my mummy? Are you my mummy? No, I'm not your mummy. Yes, I'm your mummy. Here's your lunch! chick, cat, dog, mouse, duck, sheep, hen, worm, Cheep, cheep! Miaow! Woof, woof! Squeak, squeak! Quack, quack! Baa! Cluck, cluck!*
Age	3–5
Time	5 minutes
Materials	Cut-outs of animals from the story, made from card (egg, chick, cat, dog, mouse, duck, sheep, hen and worm), sticky tack. See page 93 or the website for templates. Optional: Animal puppets or soft toys (see *Variation 3*), yellow card, sticky tape and felt-tip pens for making finger puppets (see *Extension ideas*).
Preparation	Before telling the story, stick the cut-out of the egg and the other animal cut-outs in a row on the board, as shown in the picture below. Leave enough space to place the chick between each animal. Hide the mother hen and worm cut-outs (e.g. in your pocket). Read the story and practise telling it.

Procedure

1   Get children settled for story time.
2   Position the cut-outs of the egg, chick, cat, dog, mouse, duck and sheep in a row on the board (as shown in the picture below) using sticky tack. Leave a space between each animal so that the chick can be placed there.

Figure 4.1: Position of the cut-outs on the board at the beginning of the story

3   Tell the story, changing your voice for each animal, as indicated below. As you speak, move the cut-out chick on the board so it is in front of each animal (see directions in brackets).

You:	*Crick – crack!*	(open the egg and move the chick as if it is hatching)
Chick:	*Cheep, cheep! I'm hungry! Where's my mummy? Where's my mummy?*	(sound curious) (place the chick cut-out next to the cat on the board, as if they are talking)
	Are you my mummy?	(sound hopeful)

Cat:	*Miaow! No, I'm not your mummy!*	
Chick:	*Where's my mummy?*	(place the chick cut-out next to the dog, as if they are talking)
	Are you my mummy?	(sound hopeful)
Dog:	*Woof, woof! No, I'm not your mummy!*	
Chick:	*Where's my mummy?*	(place the chick cut-out next to the mouse)
	Are you my mummy?	(sound hopeful)
Mouse:	*Squeak, squeak! No, I'm not your mummy!*	
Chick:	*Where's my mummy?*	(place the chick cut-out next to the duck)
	Are you my mummy?	(sound more desperate)
Duck:	*Quack, quack! No, I'm not your mummy!*	
Chick:	*Where's my mummy?*	(place the chick cut-out next to the sheep)
	Are you my mummy?	(sound very, very sad)
Sheep:	*Baa! No, I'm not your mummy!*	
Chick:	*Where's my mummy?*	(sound tearful)
You:	*Listen!*	
Mother hen:	*Cluck, cluck! Cluck, cluck!*	(bring out the cut-out hen and place it next to the chick)
Chick:	*Are you my mummy?*	(sound hopeful)
Mother hen:	*Yes! I'm your mummy! And here's your lunch!*	(put the cut-out worms on the board)
Chick:	*Yummy, yummy!*	(rub your tummy)
	Thank you, Mummy!	(invite the children to repeat)

4 Tell the story again. Encourage the children to repeat the animal sounds. Gradually older children will join in with some of the words or chunks of language from the story.

Variations

1 Choose volunteers to take turns being the chick, asking *Are you my mummy?* while the class takes the part of the other animals (e.g. *Miaow! No, I'm not your mummy!*).

2 With younger children, tell a shorter version with three animals (e.g. the cat, dog and mouse).

3 Tell the story using animal hand puppets or soft toys instead of the cut-outs. The puppets do not have to be the same as the animals in the story (although there must be a baby animal and its mother). Change the animals and sounds according to the puppets or soft toys available to you. The children can help to retell the story using the puppets: one child is the baby animal and another the mother; the other children act out the characters as you tell the story together.

Extension ideas

- Children make their own story board using the template provided. Reduce the number of animals to cat, dog and mouse. Photocopy one set of animals for each child. Children colour and cut out the animals. They glue the cat, dog and mouse in a row on a piece of A4 paper, leaving space to place the chick next to each animal. Once children have made their story board, tell the story together. Children move the chick in front of the cat, dog and mouse, asking *Are you my mummy?* and saying *No*. Finally they ask the hen, who says *Yes!*

- Older children can draw their own pictures for the story.
- Children make a finger puppet chick as shown below. Cut out two pieces of yellow card per child (picture 1). Stick the sides together with tape (picture 2). Children add eyes and a beak with black and orange felt-tip pens (picture 3). They move the finger puppet to talk to the other animals as they tell the story.

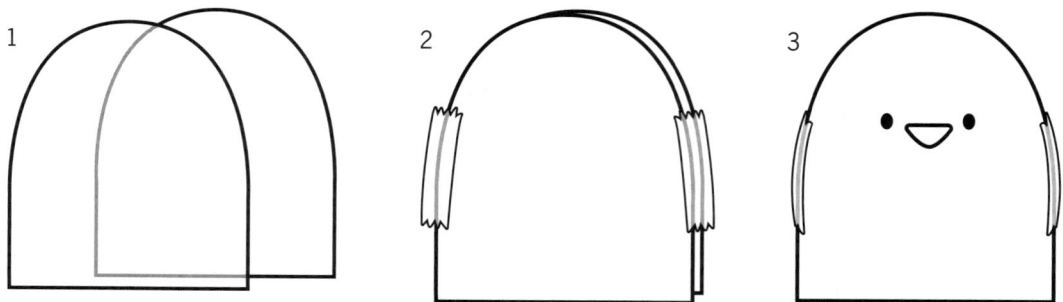

Figure 4.2: How to make a finger puppet chick

Note
If the children make a story board or a finger puppet, they can tell their parents the story at home.

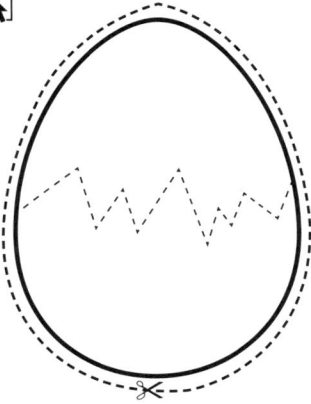

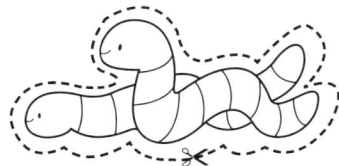

From *Activities for Very Young Learners* © Cambridge University Press 2017

4.2 Bernadette the Bear

Outline	Children listen to a story about a bear who rescues a bird and follow it with the help of pictures, repetition, mime and gestures.
Focus	*bear, happy, monkey, blackbird, tree, sing, baby bird, river, Help! Thank you.* *Can you (climb trees)? No, I can't. You can't (climb trees)? Bernadette is sad. Very sad.*
Age	4–7
Time	15–20 minutes
Materials	Pictures / flashcards of a bear, a blackbird, a monkey, a river and a tree.
Preparation	Prepare the pictures or practise drawing the items above. Read the story and practise telling it (with actions).

Procedure

1 Get children settled for story time.
2 Draw a tree on the board or show a flashcard.
3 Say *Look! A tree.* Get the children to repeat the word several times and stretch their arms up like branches.
4 Then say *Let's climb the tree.* Mime climbing a tree and get children to copy you.
5 Draw a river next to the tree or show a picture.

Figure 4.3: Tree and river pictures to copy on the board

6 Say *Look! A river.* Get children to repeat the word several times and mime a river flowing.
7 Tell the story below, using mime, gesture and drawings on the board (as shown in brackets).

This is Bernadette the Bear.	(draw or show a picture of a bear)
She is happy.	(look happy and smile)
She meets her friends.	
Matt the Monkey	(draw or show a picture of a monkey)
and Bella the Blackbird.	(draw or show a picture of a blackbird)
'Bernadette, can you climb trees?' says Matt.	(mime climbing a tree)
'No I can't,' says Bernadette.	(shake your head)
'You can't climb trees?	(mime climbing a tree)
'Ha! Ha! Ha!'	(use an arrogant, unkind tone)
says Matt the monkey.	
Bernadette is sad. Very sad.	(look sad and use a sad tone)
'Bernadette, can you sing?' says Bella.	(sing a few notes)
'No I can't,' says Bernadette.	(shake your head)
'You can't sing?	(sing a few notes)
'He! He! He!'	(use an arrogant, unkind tone)
says Bella the blackbird.	
Bernadette is sad. Very sad.	(look sad and use a sad tone)
Oh! What's that? A baby bird.	(draw a picture of a baby bird or show a picture)
It has fallen into the river.	(point at an imaginary spot in the river picture and look very shocked / worried)
'Help! Help!' say Matt and Bella.	(jump up and down and shout as if asking for help)
Bernadette jumps into the river.	(mime jumping into the river)
She helps the baby bird get out.	(mime pulling the baby bird out of the water)
Matt is happy.	(look happy and smile)
Bella is happy.	(look happy and smile)
'Thank you, Bernadette!' they say.	

8   Tell the story again several times. Encourage the children to copy your actions and expressions. Gradually the children will join in with some of the words or chunks of language from the story.

Extension idea

Once older children are familiar with the story and at ease with joining in, ask them which other animal friends could be in the story, and what they would ask Bernadette. The children will reply in their own language. Help them express their ideas in English. Some ideas for new animal friends are Linda the Lion (*Can you run very fast?*) and Peter the Parrot (*Can you fly?*).

4.3 The Monster and the Mouse

Outline	Children listen to a story about a hungry monster and a brave mouse. They participate by playing musical instruments to represent the two characters.
Focus	*monster, mouse, loud, quiet, happy, Come here, mouse. I'm hungry! Oh no! book, chair, table, toe, Ssh! Mouse is reading.*
Age	4–7
Time	5 minutes
Materials	A toy mouse with a long tail, a book, a chair, a table. A musical instrument for each child (e.g. tambourines, clackers, shakers, drums). If you haven't got instruments, you can still tell the story (the children can make noises themselves).
Preparation	Read the story and practise telling it (with the actions).

Procedure

1 Put the chair and the table in your storytelling area.

2 Get children settled for story time. Elicit or pre-teach *mouse, book, chair* and *table* by pointing to the objects.

3 Stand on one side of the storytelling area (your 'monster spot'). In a deep voice, say *I'm a monster. A big, big monster!* Make monster noises. Say *I'm hungry!* Rub your tummy.

4 Give a musical instrument to each child. Say *I'm a monster! Make a big monster noise.* Children play their instruments very loudly.

5 Move to a different place in the storytelling area to show that you are changing character (your 'mouse spot'). In a small, quiet voice, say *I'm a mouse. A very small mouse.* Make squeaking noises.

6 Point to the musical instruments and say *Make a small mouse noise.* Children play their instruments very quietly.

7 Open the book and place the toy mouse on it. Tell the story below, changing position and encouraging the children to join in by playing their musical instruments (as shown in brackets).

You:	*Look at the mouse.*	(point to the toy mouse)
	The mouse is reading. She's happy.	(children play their instruments quietly)

(Move to your 'monster spot'.)

Monster:	*I'm a monster! I'm hungry!*	(children play their instruments loudly)

You:	*Suddenly, the monster sees the mouse.*	(rub your tummy and lick your lips)
Monster:	*Hello, mouse. Come here! I'm hungry.*	(children play their instruments loudly)

(Move to your 'mouse spot'.)

Mouse:	*Oh no! Oh no!*	(children play their instruments quietly)

(Hide the toy mouse under the book, but with its tail showing.)

Monster:	*I can see you, mouse!*	
	Come here! I'm hungry!	(children play their instruments loudly)

| Mouse: | *Oh no! Oh no!* | (children play their instruments quietly) |

(Hide the toy mouse under the chair with its tail showing.)

Monster:	*I can see you, mouse!*	
	Come here! I'm hungry!	(children play their instruments loudly)
Mouse:	*Oh no! Oh no!*	(children play their instruments quietly)

(Hide the toy mouse under the table with its tail showing.)

| Monster (impatiently): | *I can see you, mouse!* | |
| | *Come here! I'm hungry!* | (children play their instruments loudly) |

(Move the toy mouse, timidly, near your foot while children play their instruments quietly. Then, pretending to be the mouse, mime biting.)

| Monster: | *Ouch! Ouch! My toe!* | (children play their instruments loudly and repeat *Ouch! Ouch!*) |
| You: | *The monster runs away.* | (run away) |

(Come back and put the toy mouse on the book.)

| You: | *The mouse is reading.* | |
| | *She's happy. Ssh!* | (children play their instruments quietly) |

Extension idea

Get a child to be the monster and another to be the mouse. They act out the story as you tell it. Divide the rest of the class into two groups. One group only plays their instruments when the monster moves or talks (loudly) and the other only plays when the mouse moves (quietly). Repeat the story, with different children as the monster and the mouse, and swapping the groups.

Note

Getting children to play instruments also works well with the traditional tale *The Three Billy Goats Gruff*. Children make a very soft noise for the baby goat, a medium noise for the mother goat and a loud noise for the father goat. They roar and play their instruments loudly when the troll comes out from under the bridge.

4.4 Greedy Gregg

Outline	Children listen to a story about a greedy boy and follow it with the help of pictures, repetition, mime and gestures.
Focus	*pizza, soup, chocolate, stomach ache, Ouch! (Timmy) is hungry, Please give me (some soup), Gregg is greedy, He eats all three (pizzas). I'm sorry.*
Age	4–7
Time	15 minutes
Materials	Pictures of pizza, a bowl of tomato soup, a bar of chocolate.
Preparation	Prepare the pictures or practise drawing the items above. Read the story and practise telling it (with actions).

Procedure

1   Get children settled for story time. Elicit or pre-teach *pizza, soup* and *chocolate* using pictures or mime (mime cutting up and eating pizza, eating soup with a spoon and breaking a bar of chocolate and eating it).

2   Draw a simple picture of a boy on the board. Ask *What's his name?* Let children call out various names. Then say *This is Gregg. Greedy Gregg.*

3   Draw a boy and a girl next to Gregg (but leave space on one side of Gregg). Say *Look. These are Gregg's friends. Timmy and Anna.*

4   Say *Gregg has got three pizzas.* Draw three pizzas near Gregg. Say *He's got three bowls of soup.* Draw three bowls near Gregg. Say *And he's got three bars of chocolate.* Draw three chocolate bars near Gregg.

5   Tell the story below, using mime, actions and drawings (as shown in brackets).

Timmy is hungry.	(mime being hungry, e.g. rub your stomach)
He says, 'Please give me a pizza.'	(point to the pizza picture / mime eating pizza)
Anna is hungry too.	(mime being hungry)
She says, 'Please give me a pizza.'	(point to the pizza picture / mime eating pizza)
But Gregg is greedy.	(frown and mime grabbing food)
He eats all three pizzas.	(erase the three pizzas from the board)
Timmy is very hungry.	(mime being very hungry)
He says, 'Please give me some soup.'	(point to the soup picture / mime eating soup)
Anna is very hungry too.	(mime being very hungry)
She says, 'Please give me some soup.'	(point to the soup picture / mime eating soup)
But Gregg is greedy.	(frown and mime grabbing food)
He eats all three bowls of soup.	(erase the bowls of soup from the board)
Timmy is soooo hungry.	(mime being extremely hungry)
He says, 'Please give me some chocolate.'	(point to the chocolate / mime eating it)
Anna is soooo hungry too.	(mime being extremely hungry)
She says, 'Please give me some chocolate.'	(point to the chocolate / mime eating it)
But Gregg is greedy.	(frown and mime grabbing food)
He eats all three bars of chocolate.	(erase the bars of chocolate from the board)

But now Gregg has got a stomach ache.	(mime having stomach ache)
He says 'Ouch! My stomach.	
I'm sorry, Timmy.	(look very sorry)
I'm sorry Anna.	
Ouch!'	(mime having stomach ache)

6 Ask the children to stand up. Tell the story again, encouraging them to copy your mimes and gestures. Gradually the children will join in with some of the words or chunks of language.

Extension idea

Tell the story again with mistakes. For example, point to the drawing of Gregg and say *This is George. Greedy George.* Encourage the children to call out *No!*, knock on their desk or clap their hands whenever they notice a mistake. Stop and ask *What's the problem?* The children give the correct information (e.g. *Gregg!*). Say *Oops! Oh yes. I'm sorry* and repeat the sentence with the correct wording (e.g. *This is Gregg. Greedy Gregg.*) Continue in this way through the whole story.

💡 **Tip**

When you retell a story with intentional errors, as long as you welcome the children's corrections and laugh at your own mistakes, they will love correcting you, and will often find your 'mistakes' extremely amusing. It is also a way to encourage more reserved children to participate, as everyone loves to prove the teacher wrong!

4.5 Miranda the Magician

Outline	Children listen to a story about a magician and follow it with the help of pictures, gestures, rhythm and rhyme.
Focus	*magician, magic wand, pot, banana, ice cream, coffee, drink (v), fly, night, land (v), happy, Abracadabra! Cold and hot! Let's put (bananas) in the pot! Wizzy, wizzy woo! I can fly and so can you.*
Age	4–7
Time	15–20 minutes
Materials	Pictures of a large pot, bananas, ice cream, coffee, the moon and stars. Optional: A magic wand (see 5.1 *Make a magic wand*).
Preparation	Prepare pictures of the items above or practise drawing them on the board. Photocopy the picture of Miranda the Magician (see page 102) or copy it on the board. Read the story and practise telling it (with actions).

Procedure

1 Get children settled for story time. Draw a picture on the board of a girl holding a magic wand, standing next to a large pot or show the picture of Miranda the Magician (see page 102).

2 Say *This is Miranda. Miranda's a magician. Look, she's got a magic wand. Abracadabra!* (point at the wand in the picture or show a real wand) *And she's got a magic pot. A big pot.* (point at the pot)

3 Introduce / revise the other key words in the story: *banana, ice cream, coffee, moon, stars.*

4 Tell the story below, using mime and gesture (as shown in brackets).

This is Miranda. She's a Magician.	(point at the picture again)
Miranda takes a pot. A big pot.	(point to the picture of the pot or use your hands to mime 'pot')
"Abracadabra! Cold and hot! Let's put bananas in the pot!"	(mime waving a magic wand, peeling a banana and putting it in a pot, then stirring the pot)
"Abracadabra! Cold and hot! Let's put ice cream in the pot!"	(mime waving a magic wand, scooping out ice cream and putting it in a pot, then stirring the pot)
"Abracadabra! Cold and hot! Let's put coffee in the pot!"	(mime waving a magic wand, pouring coffee in the pot, then stirring)
Miranda drinks from the pot.	(mime picking up the pot and drinking from it)
She can fly.	(mime flying)
It's night.	
She can see the moon and the stars.	(draw or show pictures of the moon and stars)
Miranda is cold.	(mime shivering with cold)
She drinks from the pot again.	(mime drinking from the pot)
Miranda goes down and lands.	(mime swooping down from the sky and landing)
She is happy, and sings,	(sing the following two lines happily)
"Abracadabra! Wizzy, wizzy woo! I can fly and so can you!"	

5 Tell the story again, encouraging the children to do the mimes and actions with you. Repeat this several times (you could do this over consecutive lessons). Gradually the children will join in with some of the words as well as doing the actions.

Extension ideas
- The children make magic wands (see 5.1 *Make a magic wand* on page 116). They wave the wands at the appropriate points in the story.
- Tell the story again, leaving gaps. Use mime and gestures to elicit the missing words, for example:

Teacher:	*This is Miranda. She's a ….*	(mime waving a magic wand)
Children:	*magician*	
Teacher:	*Very good. She's a magician.*	
	Miranda takes a ….	(mime the shape of the pot)
Children:	*pot*	
Teacher:	*Yes, She takes a pot. A…*	(indicate 'big' by stretching your arms out)
Children:	*big*	
Teacher:	*A big pot! Yes.*	

- The children make their own 'magic pot'. Each child draws the outline of a large pot, chooses two or three of their favourite foods and draws them inside the pot. Check that the children know the English words for their chosen foods. Then they present their ideas to the class, e.g. *Abracadabra, cold and hot. I put apples and cornflakes in my pot.*

Note
We learned this story from Günter Gerngross, Herbert's co-author on *Super Safari* (Cambridge University Press, 2015).

PHOTOCOPIABLE

4.6 Going to Timbuktu

Outline	Children listen to a story about feelings, follow it and join in with the help of repetition and movement.
Focus	*elephant, monkey, snake, crocodile, party, dance, go to bed, happy, scared, angry, sad, tired, I / We walk and walk and walk. Then we see a (monkey). The (monkey)'s (scared). Don't be (scared)! Come with me / us to Timbuktu.*
Age	5–7
Time	15–20 minutes
Materials	Pictures or drawings of an elephant, a monkey, a snake, a crocodile. Optional: Flashcards showing feelings *happy, scared, angry, sad, tired*.
Preparation	Read the story and practise telling it (with actions and mime).

Procedure

1 Get children settled for story time. Teach / revise *elephant, monkey, snake* and *crocodile* using pictures, drawings on the board and mime. If the animal words are not new to your class, present feelings *happy, sad, scared, angry*. If they are new, teach the feelings as you tell the story.

2 Tell the first part of the story below, using mime and gesture (as shown in brackets).

I'm an elephant.	(mime being an elephant)
I'm going to Timbuktu	(walk on the spot)
and I'm happy.	(smile and mime being happy)
And I walk and walk and walk.	(keep walking on the spot)
Then I see a monkey.	(point at a spot a few metres away, then mime being a monkey)
The monkey's scared.	(look scared and mime trembling with fear)
I say, 'Don't be scared!	
Come with me to Timbuktu.'	(gesture to invite the monkey to come with you)
'OK,' says the monkey.	(make an OK gesture)
And we walk and walk and walk.	(walk on the spot)
I (the happy elephant), and the	(mime being an elephant)
scared monkey.	(mime being a monkey)
We walk and walk and walk.	(walk on the spot)

3 Repeat this part of the story, encouraging the children to stand up and join in with the actions.

4 Ask the children to sit down again, and continue with the next part of the story:

Then we see a snake.	(point at a spot a few metres away, mime being a snake)
The snake's angry.	(mime being angry)
I say, 'Don't be angry!	
Come with us to Timbuktu.'	(gesture to invite the snake to come with you)
'OK,' says the snake.	(make an OK gesture)
And we walk and walk and walk.	(walk on the spot)
I (the happy elephant),	(mime being an elephant)
the scared monkey,	(mime being a monkey)
and the angry snake.	(mime being a snake)
We walk, and walk and walk.	(walk on the spot)

5 Start the story again from the very beginning. The children stand up and join in with the actions.

6 Ask the children to sit down again, and tell the last part of the story:

Then we see a crocodile.	(point at a spot a few metres away, mime being a crocodile)
The crocodile's sad.	(mime being sad)
I say, 'Don't be sad!	
Come with us to Timbuktu.'	(gesture to invite the crocodile to come with you)
'OK,' says the crocodile.	(make an OK gesture)
And we walk and walk and walk.	(walk on the spot)
I (the happy elephant),	(mime being a happy elephant)
the scared monkey,	(mime being a scared monkey)
the angry snake,	(mime being an angry snake)
and the sad crocodile.	(mime being a sad crocodile)
We walk, and walk and walk.	(walk on the spot)
And here we are in Timbuktu.	
We have a party	(jump up and down happily)
and dance rock'n'roll.	(dance on the spot)
And then we are tired.	(mime being tired)
And we go to bed.	(mime going to bed / sleep)

7 Tell the story again from the beginning. The children stand up and join in with the actions.

Extension ideas

- If you take five minutes in several consecutive lessons to perform the story together, you should notice that the children will begin to speak the words along with you, as well as doing the actions.
- With older children, during the story, explore the feelings *happy, scared, angry* and *sad* by asking, e.g. *Why is monkey scared?* When a child volunteers a reason in their own language add it to the story in English, e.g. *Monkey's scared because there's a hunter behind the tree. Don't be scared! Come with us to Timbuktu!*

Note
Herbert learned this story from Erich Ballinger.

4.7 The Butterfly finger play

Outline	Children act out a non-fiction story about the life cycle of a butterfly, through a finger play.
Focus	*butterfly, leaf, egg, caterpillar, eats and eats, another leaf, tree (branch), cocoon, fly, beautiful*
Age	4–7
Time	5 minutes
Materials	None
Preparation	If possible, show children a video or read a book about the life cycle of a butterfly. If not, draw pictures showing the life cycle of a butterfly on the board.

Procedure

1 Get children settled for story time.
2 Entwine your thumbs with your palms flat to make the shape of a butterfly. Flutter your fingers as if they were the wings of the butterfly (see picture below). Ask *Can you be a butterfly?* The children practise making the butterfly shape with their fingers.

Figure 4.4: The butterfly

3 Tell the story of a butterfly's life cycle using the finger play techniques (shown in brackets).

This butterfly is going to lay an egg…	
here on this leaf	(hold your left palm flat with your index finger resting in the centre of your palm)
	Where is your leaf?
Where is your egg?	(children copy you)
Here is the egg.	(curl your palm around your index finger)

Figure 4.5: The egg on the leaf

Listen and look.
Can you see? The egg is opening.
Here is a caterpillar!   (open your left hand and wriggle your right index finger)
Look! The caterpillar eats the egg.
Eat the egg on the leaf, everyone. Now the caterpillar is eating the leaf.
Yum, yum, yum.   (wriggle your index finger 'caterpillar' over the surface of your palm)

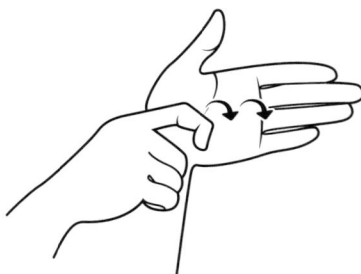

Figure 4.6: The caterpillar eating the leaf

Now the caterpillar is eating another leaf.
Yum, yum, yum.   (close your palm and then open it again, as if it's a different leaf;
                                          wriggle your index finger 'caterpillar' over your palm, repeat
                                          three or four times)
The caterpillar is eating another leaf… and another. Yum, yum, yum!

Now the caterpillar is very full.   (slow down as if you are getting very full)
The caterpillar is climbing a tree.   (hold your right arm up with your wrist bent and your fingers
                                          curved around like branches. Wriggle your caterpillar finger up
                                          the tree trunk and then hang your caterpillar finger downwards
                                          between your two branch fingers on your left hand)

Figure 4.7: The caterpillar climbing a tree

Look. The caterpillar is making a cocoon. (wrap your left hand around your caterpillar finger)

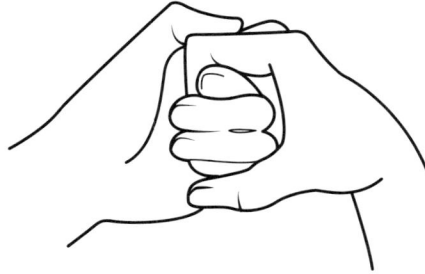

Figure 4.8: The caterpillar inside its cocoon

> *The caterpillar is inside the cocoon. It's very sleepy.*
> *But look! It's moving!*   (wriggle your finger inside the 'cocoon')

4   Open your hands, entwine your thumbs to make a butterfly as you did at the start and flutter your fingers as if they were wings. Say *And here is a beautiful butterfly. Fly, butterfly, fly!*

Extension idea

Children make a butterfly with a peg and paper wings (see 5.10 *A handprint tree with butterflies*). They choose a bead or a button for an egg, cut leaves out of green paper, and make a cocoon by wrapping cotton wool inside a paper cupcake case. Children point to each thing they have made as you talk about the life cycle of the butterfly.

Note

Many traditional finger plays can be found in books and on the internet, including *Five little ducks, Five speckled frogs, Grandma's glasses* and *Insy winsy spider*. See also 3.2 *Ten little bugs* (page 71).

4.8 At the dentist's

Outline	Children watch and take part in a sketch about going to the dentist's.
Focus	*dentist, ice cream, lollies, chocolate, sweet, Good morning. Thank you. Do you like…? Yes, I do. No, thanks!*
Age	6–7
Time	15–20 minutes
Materials	A picture of a dentist, a picture of ice cream, real lollipops, chocolate and sweets or pictures of lollipops, chocolate and sweets. Optional: A white coat or shirt.
Preparation	Practise the sketch so you can perform it without reading the words.

Procedure

1   Get children settled for story time. Put a chair at the front of the class. Show a picture of a dentist, or mime being a dentist by asking children to open their mouths and pretending to look at their teeth. Put on a white coat or shirt if you have one and say *I'm a dentist*.

2   Ask a child to come to the front. Say *Good morning*. Get the child to repeat this. Then say *Sit down, please*. Prompt the child to sit down and say *Thank you*.

3   Say *Open your mouth*. Act looking at the child's teeth (like a dentist). Say *OK. Thank you. That's fine*. Wait for the child to stand up. Say *Goodbye*. Encourage the child to reply.

4   Repeat this several times, with different children coming to the front.

5   Ask a confident child to come to the front. Prompt / help the child to act out the following sketch with you (actions in brackets). Start by saying *I'm the dentist* again.

> Dentist: *Good morning.*
> Child: *Good morning.*
> Dentist: *Sit down, please. Open your mouth.*
> (child opens mouth, dentist checks the child's teeth)
> Dentist: (looks worried) *Mmm … Do you like ice cream?* (show a picture of ice cream)
> Child: *Yes, I do.*
> Dentist: *Do you like lollies?* (show a picture of lollies or real lollies)
> Child: *Yes, I do.*
> Dentist: *Do you like chocolate?* (show a picture of chocolate or real chocolate)
> Child: *Yes, I do.*
> Dentist: (acting as if using a dentist's drill, and making an appropriate noise) *It's OK now.*
> Child: *Thank you!*
> Dentist: (offering the child a real sweet or miming) *A sweet?*
> Child: *No, thanks!*

6   Ask the class to give a big round of applause to the child. Repeat several times with different children.

Extension idea
Once the children are at ease with acting out the patient's role, ask a confident child to be the dentist. As that role has more language, you need to be prepared to help the child by prompting, e.g. standing behind the child and whispering the lines when needed.

Note
The sketch above is based on an idea by Günter Gerngross, Herbert's co-author on *Super Safari* (Cambridge University Press, 2015).

4.9 The Enormous Turnip

Outline	Children listen to a traditional Russian folktale and join in with the actions and words.
Focus	*seed, man, woman, girl, boy, dog, mouse, water (v), wait, turnip, hungry, (very) big, soup, (The plant) grows and grows. The (woman) holds onto the (man). (The man) pulls and pulls. / They pull and pull. Can I help? Yes, please. / No!*
Age	3–7
Time	5 minutes for the story, 20–30 minutes for the craft activity (see *Extension ideas*).
Materials	A story book of *The Enormous Turnip* with pictures (it doesn't need to be in English), a real seed or picture of a seed, pictures of a plant (if possible several pictures of the plant as it grows). If you do not have a story book, use the character templates from the website, sticky tack. Optional: Character templates, crayons, scissors, and glue (see *Extension ideas*).
Preparation	Prepare the character cut-outs by photocopying the templates on page 113 or downloading them from the website. Read the story and practise telling it with a storybook or using the pictures.

Procedure

1 Get children settled for story time. Introduce the main characters in the story before you start, using the story book, the cut-outs or generic pictures of a man, a woman, a girl, a boy, a dog and a mouse.

2 Show a real seed (or a picture of one) and ask *What's this? … It's a seed. It's a tiny seed!*

3 Tell the story below, changing your voice for the different characters and using actions and pictures (shown in brackets):

This is a man. This is a woman.	(show or draw pictures of the man and the woman)
The man plants the seed.	(mime making a hole and planting a seed)
And the woman waters it.	(mime watering the seed with a watering can)
The man and the woman wait.	
They wait and wait.	(cross your arms and tap your feet, looking at the spot where you 'planted' the seed)
What's this? It's a plant. It's a turnip.	(show or draw a picture of a small plant)
The plant grows and grows! And it grows and grows!	
	(show or draw a picture of a bigger plant and mime looking up at the growing plant)
It grows and grows! It's very big!	(look amazed)
The man and the woman look at the turnip.	
"I'm hungry," says the woman.	
The man says "I'm hungry."	(rub your tummy and put the picture of the man on the board next to the picture of the plant)
The man pulls. He pulls and pulls.	(mime pulling at a plant in the ground)
But the turnip doesn't move!	(shake your head)
"Can I help?" says the woman.	(show the picture of the woman)

The woman holds onto the man.	(put the picture of the woman behind the picture of the man on the board)
They pull and pull!	(mime pulling at a plant in the ground)
But the turnip doesn't move.	(shake your head)
Here comes a girl.	(show the picture of a girl)
"Can I help?" says the girl.	
"Yes, please!" say the man and the woman.	
The girl holds onto the woman and the woman holds onto the man.	(put the picture of the girl on the board behind the woman)
They pull and pull!	(mime pulling at the plant)
But the turnip doesn't move.	(shake your head)
Here comes a boy.	(show the picture of a boy)
"Can I help?" says the boy.	
"Yes, please!" say the man and the woman and the girl.	
The boy holds onto the girl and the girl holds onto the woman and the woman holds onto the man.	
	(put the picture of the boy on the board behind the girl)
They pull and pull!	(mime pulling)
But the turnip doesn't move.	(shake your head)
Here comes a dog.	(show the picture of a dog)
"Can I help?" says the dog.	
"Yes, please!' say the man, the woman, the girl and the boy.	
The dog holds onto the boy and the boy holds onto the girl; the girl holds onto the woman and the woman holds onto the man.	(put the picture of the dog on the board behind the boy)
They pull and pull!	(mime pulling)
But the turnip doesn't move.	(shake your head)
Here comes a mouse. A small mouse.	(show the picture of a mouse)
"Can I help?" says the mouse.	
"No!" say the man, the woman, the girl, the boy and the dog, "You're too small!"	
"Oh, please, please, can I help?" cries the mouse.	
"Well, OK," they say.	
The mouse holds onto the dog; the dog holds onto the boy and the boy holds onto the girl; the girl holds onto the woman and the woman holds onto the man.	
	(put the picture of the mouse behind the picture of the girl)
They pull and pull!	
They pull and they pull!	(mime pulling with a lot of effort)
And suddenly… POP! The turnip comes out of the ground!	(mime pulling the turnip out)
"Hooray!" they say.	(jump up and down)
The old man and the old woman cut up the turnip and they put it in a pot.	
	(mime cutting the turnip and putting the pieces in a pot)

They stir and stir…	(mime stirring a lot of soup)
And make a delicious soup! Yum!	(mime eating delicious soup from a bowl with a spoon)
"Thank you!" say the girl, the boy,	
the dog and the mouse.	(rub your tummy and look very happy)

4 Tell the story again. This time encourage children to do the actions with you. They can also join in with the repeated lines, for example, *It grows and grows. Can I help? Yes, please!* and *They pull and pull!* Pause and point to each character, so that children say the names instead of you, e.g. *The … (mouse) holds onto the … (dog) and the dog holds onto the … (boy) and the … boy holds onto the… (girl). The girl holds onto the… (woman) and the woman holds onto the… (man).*

Variation

Act out the story with the children instead of using pictures. Choose six children to be the man, the woman, the boy, the girl, the dog and the mouse. The teacher is the turnip plant – the children playing the roles line up in turn behind you as you tell the story and attempt to move you by pulling. The children playing the man and woman then pretend to cut up the turnip and put it in a pot, etc. All the children act out eating the soup at the end.

Extension ideas

- Photocopy the cut-outs so there is one set for each child (see website – add ref). Children colour the pictures and cut them out. Tell the story. Children move the cut-out characters, saying as much of the story as they can. With very young children, pre-cut the pieces so that they just need to colour them.
- Tell this story in spring and then plant real seeds and watch them grow.
- Learn about root vegetables. Show children carrot, turnip and beetroot seeds. They are all very different! Stick the seeds on paper with sellotape and then ask children to draw the vegetable next to each seed. Use real vegetables or find pictures to display on the wall or your computer screen.

Note

Traditional tales which work well with very young learners often rely on repetition or have few characters. They also have a simple storyline which is easy for children to understand with the help of drawings, some key objects and clear miming. Other traditional stories you could tell in the classroom are *The Three Billy Goats Gruff, Jack and the Beanstalk, Goldilocks* and *The Little Red Hen.* You will find templates of the characters and storytelling instructions for these tales on the internet.

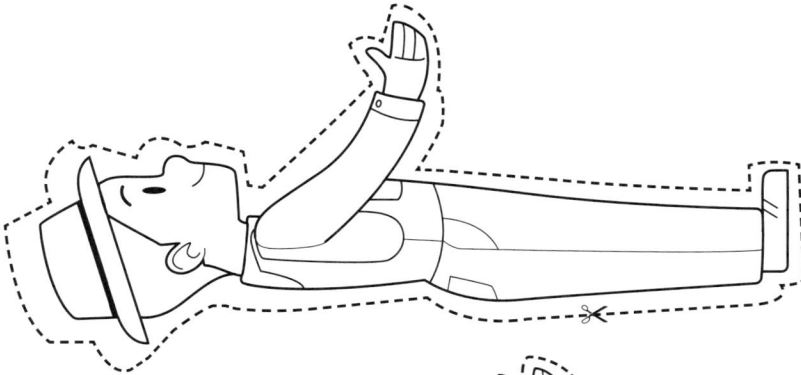

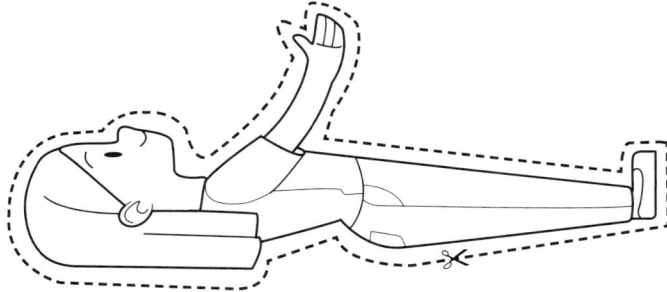

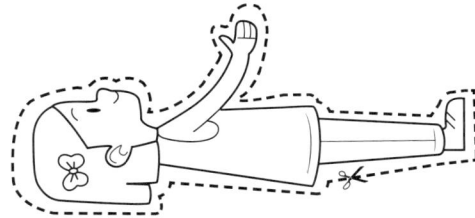

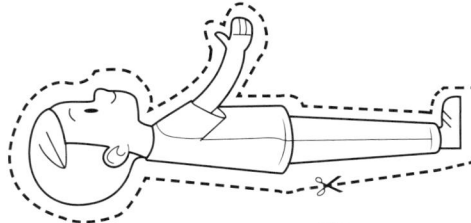

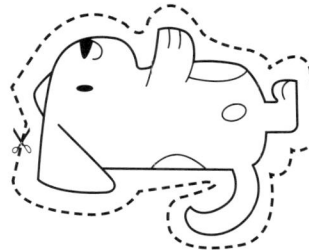

From *Activities for Very Young Learners* © Cambridge University Press 2017

PHOTOCOPIABLE

5 Arts, crafts and displays

Art and craft activities often provide moments of harmony in the very young learner classroom, since children work both independently and as part of a group. But how do we ensure that these industrious moments are also language-rich? With the help of models, demonstration and a step-by-step approach, children experience communication *in action* – an important part of their learning experience. Just as they have picked up their own language, they will gradually begin to use words and chunks of language they hear from the teacher and other children during the activity.

Choosing art and craft activities at the language and fine motor skills level of your age group will help to keep the atmosphere somewhat calm (or at least as calm as it can be when you and the children are as busy as bees!). Where possible, have an example of the completed picture or craft project so that children know what they are going to do. Make sure you only put out the materials needed for each step. It is also vital to demonstrate each step using simple language, and for this reason we have included examples of classroom talk in many of the activities, for example, *First we do this. Watch me ... like this. Yes, that's right. Cut this line, not that one.* Remember to provide plenty of individual, descriptive praise, e.g. *Wow, I like the hat on your funny face. That's a beautiful red roof, Nadia! You have put very small feet on your monster, Riley. I like that!*

Once the craft project or display has been completed, try to exploit its language potential. You will find suggestions for ways to do this in the Extension ideas after many of the activities in this chapter. Remember, too, that when children take their art work home, you create a valuable connection with their parents, who can see what the children have been doing and may even be able to talk to them about the project using some English words.

Some of the activities below require more materials and time but there are others which can be done with a minimum of fuss. We hope these ideas will provide you with enjoyable experiences in the classroom, and inspire you to look for or create your own art and craft activities too.

5.1 Make a magic wand

Outline	Children make magic wands then use them to practise language, such as following instructions, writing numbers and drawing shapes.
Focus	*magic wand, feather, straw, glue*
Age	4–6
Time	10–15 minutes
Materials	Craft feathers and paper straws (one straw and one feather for each child), glue, plastic plates / tubs.
Preparation	Make a magic wand to show the class.

Procedure

1 Show the children your magic wand. Say *This is my magic wand*, wave it in the air and say some magic words e.g. *Abracadabra, one two three, Abracadabra, look at me!* Draw numbers or shapes in the air with your wand for the children to guess.

2 Demonstrate how to make the wand. Put some glue on a plate. Dip the quill end of the feather in it then stick the feather to the straw. Say *Put the feather in the glue. Now put the feather in the top of the straw, like this.*

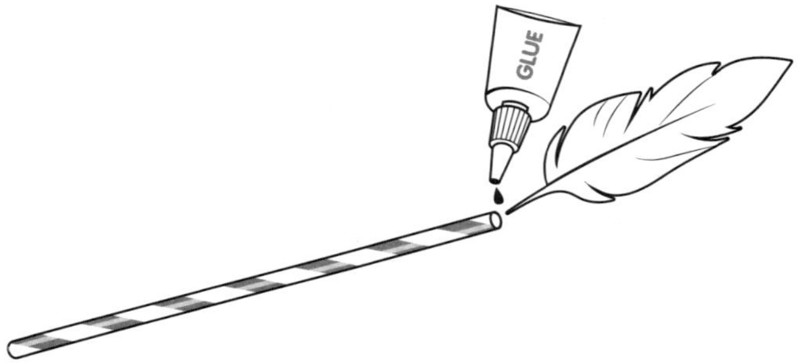

Figure 5.1: Making a magic wand

3 Hand out the feathers and straws. Ask e.g. *What colour (do you want)? The green one?*

4 Put a plate with glue on it on each table. Say *Take turns. Make magic wands.* Help the children and give more instructions, as appropriate.

5 Leave the wands to dry and then use them for games and activities (see *Extension ideas*, below).

Extension ideas

• Play pointing games. Say *Point to a circle / square / triangle* or *Point to something red / green / black / blue*. Children point to objects of the correct shape or colour with their wands.

• Stand with your back to the class. Holding the wand high above your head, draw a large number (for example, 2) slowly in the air. Ask *What number is it?* Pupils say the number together. Older children can take turns writing numbers for the others to guess.

• Children stand in rows. With your back to them, use your magic wand to make movements and shapes in the air. Give instructions at the same time, e.g. *Up, down, and around. Let's make a circle! Let's make a triangle – a big one ... and a small one!* Children copy you with their wands. You could play some music in the background.

5.2 Funny face paper plates

Outline	Children make a funny face using a cardboard circle or paper plate.
Focus	*eyes, nose, mouth, ears, hair, face, happy*
Age	3–7
Time	15–20 minutes
Materials	A cardboard circle or paper plate for each child, pre-cut shapes or shape stickers (circles, triangles), paints, crayons, coloured wool.
Preparation	Make a funny face plate to show the class.

Procedure

1 Show your funny face plate to the class. Point and ask about the different features, e.g. *What's this? That's right, it's a nose! And these? Yes, eyes! What colour are they?*
2 Draw a face on the board, showing how and where to draw eyes, a nose and a mouth. As you draw say, e.g. *Let's draw eyes. Draw them here, in the middle. My nose is under the eyes. Here's my mouth. It's a big mouth. She's happy. What colour is her hair? Yes, it's black.*
3 Distribute the paper plates or cardboard circles and materials. Children can either draw the faces or use pre-cut shapes or shape stickers (circles for the eyes, triangles for the nose). They can glue wool around the top edge for hair.
4 As children make their funny faces, comment and ask, e.g. *What are you drawing, Jamie? That's a beautiful big mouth. Well done!*
5 When the plates are finished, children can take turns to show them to the class. Older children can introduce their funny face plates, e.g. *Hello. This is Jack.* and add more information, e.g. *He's got brown eyes. He likes football.*
6 Display the funny faces in the classroom.

Variations

1 With younger children, provide pre-cut shapes or use stickers for all the parts of the face.
2 Children stick pasta pieces in a variety of shapes onto the plate to make the eyes, ears and nose. They can also paint the faces once the glue is dry (blue eyes, pink cheeks, etc.).
3 Children make clown faces on the plates. Supply pom-poms for noses, large googly eyes and foam to make into hats, bow ties, moustaches, eyebrows, etc.

Extension ideas

• At the beginning of the year, give each child a paper plate with their name on it. The plate can be used to work on (to make cleaning up easier) and to hold craft projects children are in the process of making.
• Paper plates form the basis of many great craft activities, for example, making hats (the edge of the plate makes the brim), making steering wheels (children paint the rim of the plate and add a cross in the centre) and making dioramas (e.g. a beach scene or an island).

Figure 5.2: A funny face paper plate

5.3 Our feelings wall display

Outline	Children make a face with different expressions and use it to explore and begin to understand their emotions.
Focus	*hair, eyes, nose, mouth, How do you feel today? I'm (happy / sad / scared / angry).*
Age	4–6
Time	20–30 minutes
Materials	A copy of the face and mouth cut-outs for each child (see page 121 or download from the website), four small pieces of sticky tack for each child, crayons, scissors.
Preparation	Make an example of the feelings face by photocopying page 121, writing your name and colouring the picture / adding hair and other features to make the face look like you. Cut along the first dotted line and cut out the four mouths. Put sticky tack on the back of each paper mouth.

Procedure

1 Show the children the face you have prepared. Say *This is me. This is my hair. These are my eyes and this is my nose. What's missing? That's right, my mouth!*

2 Tell the children that we are not happy all the time. Say that sometimes we are angry, we are sad or we are scared. With older children ask *How do you feel?* (children repeat). Put the happy mouth on the face and say *I'm happy* (children repeat). Mime being happy. The children copy you.

3 Repeat step 2 for the other emotions, changing the mouth on the face each time. Make sure you clearly mime each emotion for children to copy.

4 Practise the emotions by changing the mouth on your picture, miming the corresponding feeling and saying *I'm ….* Each time the children copy the mime and the sentence, e.g. *I'm angry.*

5 Give out the copies of the feelings face and crayons. Children add hair and other features to the faces (except mouths). Older children can write their names, colour their faces and the four mouths the same colour.

6 Once the decorating is completed, give out the scissors. Children cut out the four mouths.

7 Give each child four pieces of sticky tack. They put a piece of sticky tack on each of the mouths they have cut out. Tell the children to choose an emotion for their face and stick the correct mouth in the space to show it. Once they have put a mouth on the face, tell them to stick the other mouths around the face. Collect all the feelings faces.

8 Display the faces on a wall at a height children can reach. Ask children when we might feel happy, sad, angry or scared. Translate their answers into English and use mime. Say *It's OK to be sad, angry and scared. And it's great to be happy!* Tell children that when they notice their feelings change, they can go to the wall and change the mouth on their feelings face. They can do this any time when you are teaching them, not just in this lesson. In subsequent classes, ask the children *How do you feel?* and tell them to change the mouth on their feelings face if they want to.

Extension ideas

- Play a feelings game. Say *I'm happy.* The children find the happy mouth and stick it on their feelings face. Say a different emotion, e.g. *I'm sad.* The children change the mouth on their face. Repeat several times. When the children are familiar with the game, let different children take turns to lead.

- Sing the song *If you're happy and you know it* and do the actions.
- Ask the children to line up, one behind the other, with you at the front. Culture permitting, get the children to put their hands on the hips or shoulders of the person in front of them, making a conga line. Say *We're happy!* and alter your expression and the style of your movements to match the emotion. The children copy you in the conga line. Do the same for *We're angry* and *We're scared*. With older children, add more feelings, e.g. *tired* (stretch and yawn), *hungry* (rub your tummy) and *excited* (jump up and down).

💡 Tip

Try to acknowledge your children's emotions in class, so that they know it's OK to feel sad, angry and scared sometimes. You can do this non-verbally by nodding and showing understanding, or, if necessary, ask children if they'd like to tell you what's making them feel sad or angry. Resolve disputes in class while showing acceptance for the children's natural emotional reactions.

Name _____

5.4 Our counting books

Outline	Children make a book using a variety of craft techniques, in different sessions.
Focus	Numbers 1–10, *me, hands, chicks, squares, circles, triangles, trees, stars, hearts, clouds, flowers, the end*
Age	5–7
Time	20–30 minutes, over several lessons
Materials	A counting book with numbers one to ten (it doesn't have to be in English). A book made of five pieces of A4 coloured card for each child. See below for the materials for each page of the book (e.g. coloured card in different shapes, stickers, glue, crayons, scissors, finger paints, paint brushes and sponges).
Preparation	Make a blank book for each child by stapling five pieces of paper or coloured card together. Put sticky tape over the staples to form the spine of the book. Complete the relevant page of a model counting book before each session to show the class.

Procedure

1   Show children a one to ten counting book (there are many to choose from). Tell them that they are going to make their own counting book. Give each child one of your pre-made blank books.

2   Make the book, page by page, in ten different lessons. At the beginning of each session, show the children an example of the finished page. Ask questions, e.g. *What is it? What colours can you see? What shape is this? How many?* After the Procedure you will find instructions for each page.

3   Start reading the pages of the counting book after each session, so that by the time the last page is finished, the children are able to 'read' the book with you. Suggested language you could use:

> Page 1: *One me (Only one me in the whole world!)*
> Page 2: *Two hands (My hands.)*
> Page 3: *Three* (lift the flap) *chicks (in a tree)!*
> Page 4: *Four squares (What colour are they?)*
> Page 5: *Five circles (They're oranges.)*
> Page 6: *Six triangles (They're trees.)*
> Page 7: *Seven stars (in the sky.)*
> Page 8: *Eight hearts (I love you.)*
> Page 9: *Nine clouds (It's rainy today.)*
> Page 10: *Ten flowers (They're beautiful.)*
> *And that's the end!*

4   Children write the numbers on each page. If appropriate, copy the text which is not in brackets above. Use numerals instead of words (e.g. *1 me, 2 hands*). Photocopy and cut up the text so that the children can stick the phrases on the pages of their book.

5   Once children can 'read' their book, they can take it home to read to their parents.

Variations

1   Make a counting book from one to five, or complete just one of the pages as a picture on its own.

2   Change the pictures on the pages of the book to suit the topics you're covering with your class (e.g. classroom objects, animals, holidays, seasons).

3 Choose just one topic and give the book an appropriate title, e.g. *Our animals counting book /
  Our food counting book*. Each page has a different item from the topic.

Note

This project appeals to children because they are using different techniques to make the books.

Page 1: The front cover. Children decorate an oval-shaped piece of card to represent their face.
They glue the card onto the cover of the book and then write or trace their name below the face.

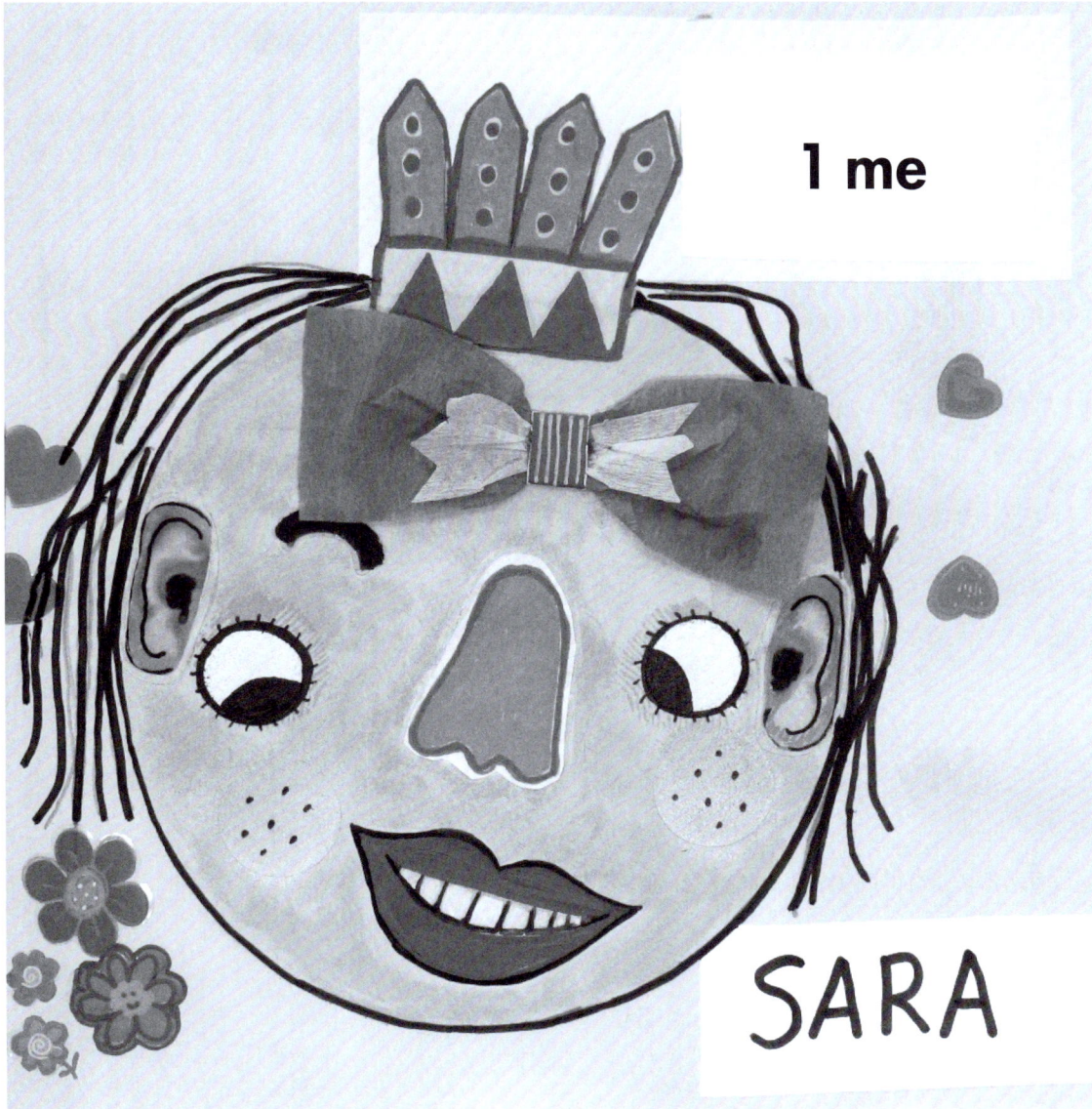

Figure 5.3: The front cover of a counting book

Page 2: 2 Children make two handprints on the page using finger paints.

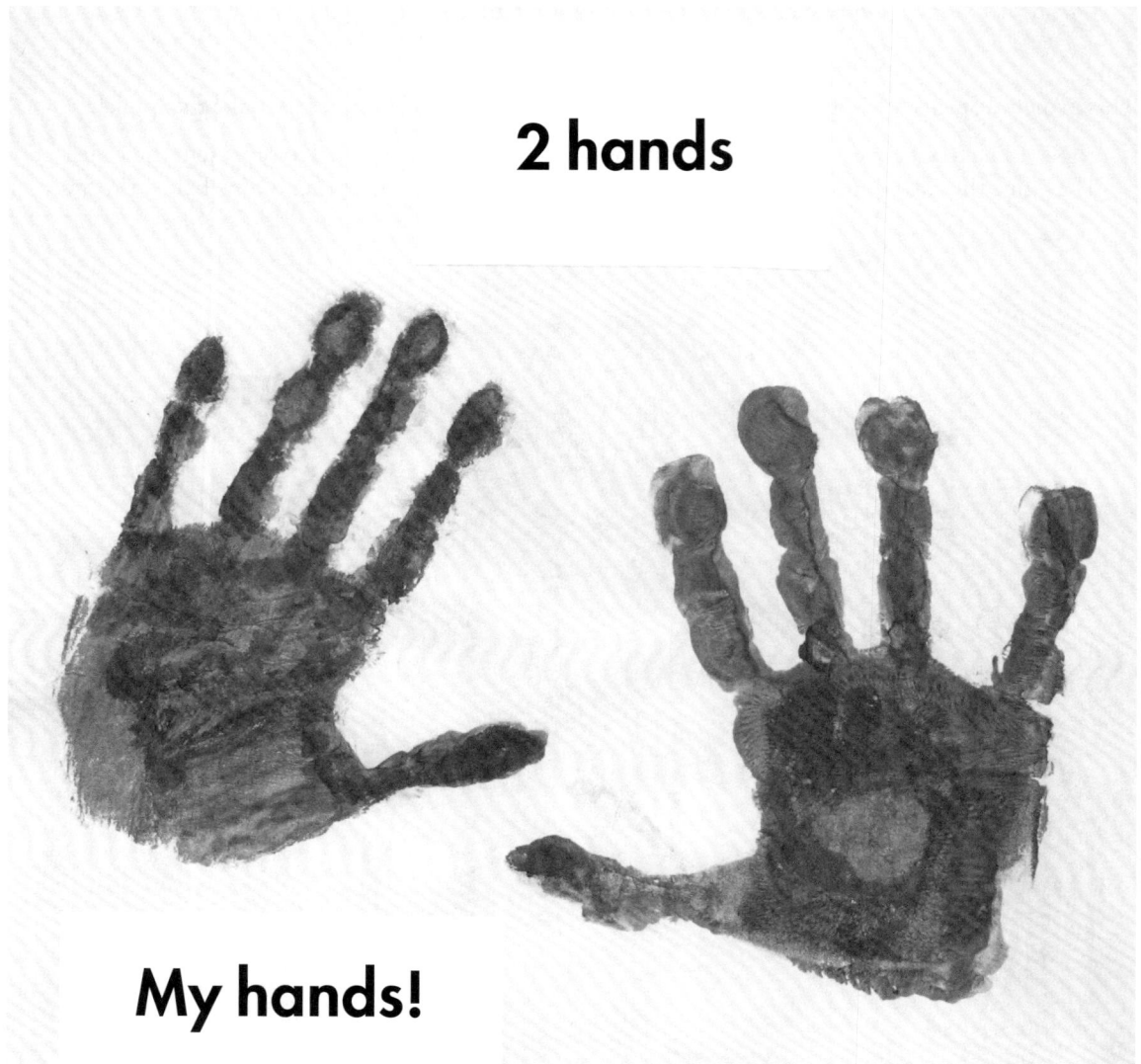

2 hands

My hands!

Figure 5.4: Page two of the counting book

Page 3: 3 Children make a picture of three chicks in a tree by drawing a trunk and a nest with brown crayon and adding three yellow thumbprints to the nest. They draw eyes and a beak on each chick. Cut out tree shapes in green card. Children glue the top of the card above the chicks (to make a flap which covers the chicks). They lift the flap to reveal the chicks.

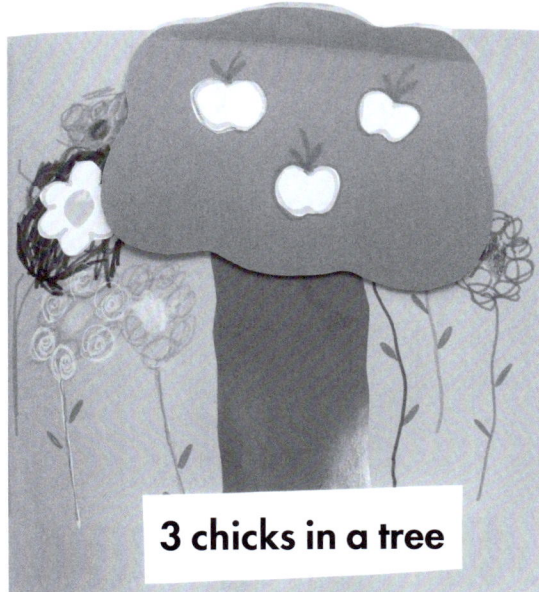

Figure 5.5: Page three of the counting book

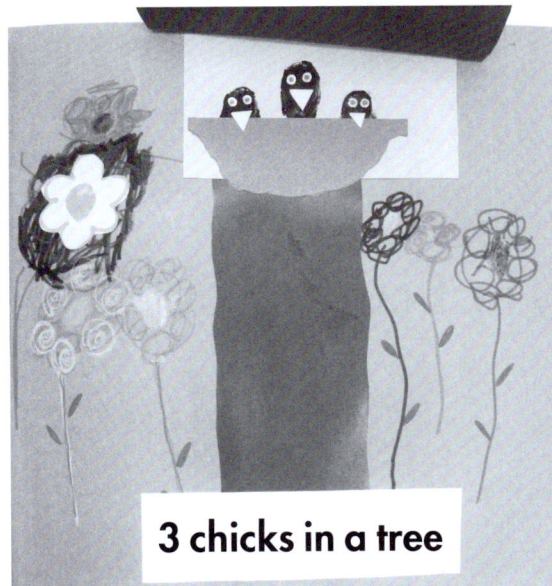

Figure 5.6: Page three showing the flap lifted

Page 4: 4 Children stick four paper squares in different colours on the page.

4 squares

What colour are they?

Figure 5.7: Page four of the counting book

Page 5: 5 Children dip sponges in paint to make orange circles. They add stems and leaves in green crayon to make oranges.

5 circles

They're oranges.

Figure 5.8: Page five of the counting book

Page 6: 6 Children stick six large green triangles on the page to make trees and add brown trunks with crayons. Early finishers can add the sun, flowers and birds.

Figure 5.9: Page six of the counting book

Page 7: 7 Children stick seven star stickers on the page. If you have time, ask them to colour the background black or dark blue before you give out the stickers.

Figure 5.10: Page seven of the counting book

Page 8: 8 Make heart-shaped potato stamps, several for each table. Put red or pink paint in a shallow dish on each table. Children stamp eight hearts on the page and then embellish them with glitter glue. They count as they stamp.

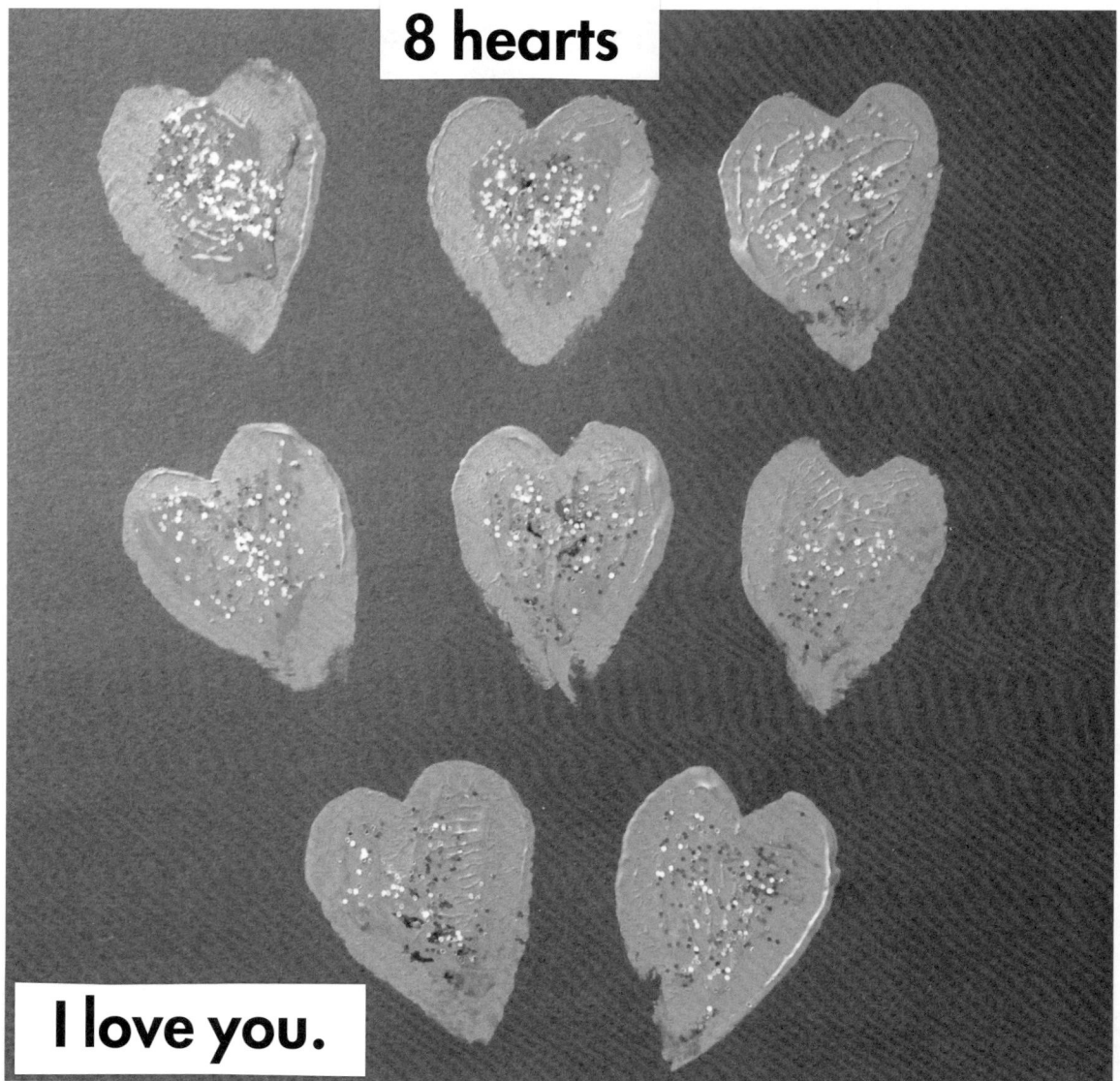

8 hearts

I love you.

Figure 5.11: Page eight of the counting book

Page 9: 9 Make cloud-shaped potato stamps for each table. Put white paint in a shallow dish. Children stamp nine clouds on the page. They count as they stamp. They add faces and rain with crayons.

Figure 5.12: Page nine of the counting book

Page 10: *10* Children glue cut-out flower shapes on the page to make ten flowers, adding stickers and decorating the flowers with crayons.

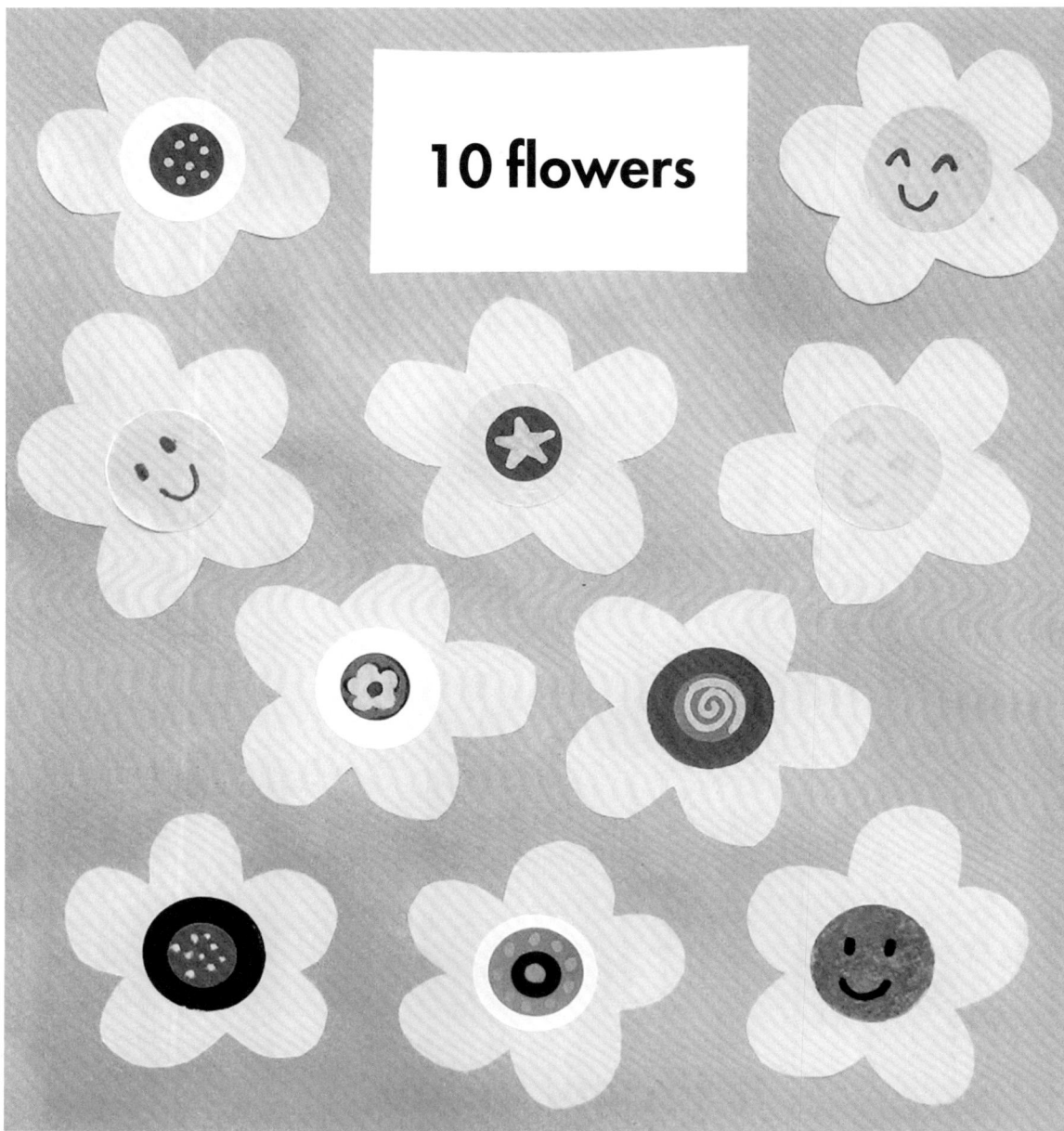

Figure 5.13: Page ten of the counting book

5.5 Paper shape town display

Outline	Children make a collage town picture using different shapes.
Focus	*square, rectangle, triangle, circle, colours, town, house, window, door, roof*
Age	4–7
Time	20–30 minutes
Materials	A piece of A4 paper with a line drawn along the bottom for each child, different coloured paper cut into shapes (squares, circles, rectangles and triangles), glue.
Preparation	Cut the paper into shapes (squares, rectangles, triangles, circles) of different sizes. Make an example of a paper shape town to show the class.

Procedure

1 Show the paper shape town you have made and say, e.g. *This is my town. Isn't it beautiful? Look, here's a small house. This is a big building. Is it a school? Can you see a big square? What colour is it? Can you see a little rectangle? Is it red or yellow?* Alternatively, draw a line to represent a street on the whiteboard, then draw a row of buildings along the line made from simple shapes (squares, rectangles, circles, triangles). Ask about the shapes and colours as you draw.

2 Say *Let's make a town.* Demonstrate how to glue the shapes on a piece of paper along the line which represents a street. Say *Look at this. What is it? A square. I'm going to stick it here and I'm going to put a triangle, a red triangle, on top.*

3 Give out pieces of paper, glue and paper shapes. Children draw a horizontal line across the paper at the bottom to show the street (with younger children, draw it for them) and make their town. They use crayons to finish it by adding windows, doors, birds, clouds, and so on. Talk to the children as they work, e.g. *What shape is that? What colour is this? Is this a house? Is it a school? Can you draw the sun, now, Ahmed? That's a lovely tree, Julia!*

4 Display the paper shape pictures in a long line, with all the street lines connected, to make a town.

Figure 5.14: An example of a paper shapes town

Variations
1   Use stickers instead of pre-cut shapes.
2   Older children can cut out their own shapes, although it is a good idea to have a selection of shapes prepared to get everyone started.
3   Children can use their imaginations to create more fanciful towns and give their town a name. They can add street signs, traffic lights, speed limit signs and even label the buildings (*toy shop, office, school*), with your help.

Extension ideas
•   Take the opportunity of this project to talk about road safety: when and where to cross a street, what to look out for, and so on.
•   Make shape pictures about other topics, for example, transport (children use the paper shapes to make cars, planes, lorries, trains, etc.).
•   Ask children to create castles, palaces or imaginary buildings from the shapes, rather than a town.

5.6 Learning to draw

Outline	Children learn how to draw simple pictures step by step.
Focus	*circle, square, oval, rectangle, Draw a line / the … (like this)*. Revision of known words, e.g. *window, door, ladybird, butterfly*.
Age	4–7
Time	5–10 minutes
Materials	A mini-whiteboard, board pen and cloth for each child (or a piece of paper and pencil).
Preparation	Choose from the pictures below or find pictures suitable for your age group and the words you want to practise on the internet. Practise drawing the pictures step by step, thinking of the language you will need to use.

Procedure

1 Give a mini-whiteboard, board pen and cloth (or a piece of blank paper and a pencil) to each child.

2 Show children how to draw an object step by step, giving clear instructions at the same time. For example, a window. Say *Can you draw a square? Watch me*. Draw a square on the whiteboard, then wait for the children to draw theirs. Draw a vertical line in the middle of the square and say *Now draw a line like this … That's right*. Draw a horizontal line saying *And another line, like this!* At each stage of the instructions, pause and look at the children's work and give them plenty of encouragement. At the end ask *What is it? It's a window. … Show me your windows. Well done, everyone!*

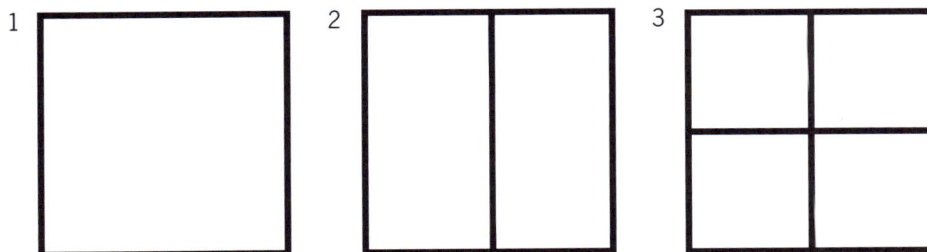

Figure 5.15: The three steps for drawing a window

3 Clean the board and say *Rub out your window, everyone* (or give out a new piece of paper).

4 Give instructions for a different picture, e.g. a door: Say Are *you ready? Now draw a rectangle. Like this. Now put a circle in the rectangle. What is it? It's a door! Show me… A door!*

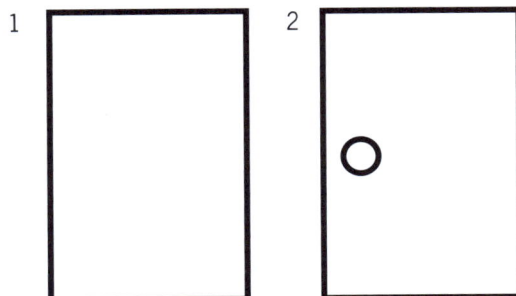

Figure 5.16: The two steps for drawing a door

5   At the end of the activity, children erase their pictures and put the whiteboards, pens and cloths away.

Variations

1   Ladybird: Say *Can you draw a ladybird? Watch me. Draw a circle… Now draw a line here, like this… . Now draw a line here and colour it… Now draw the little circles, like this… And put six legs: three here and three here. …*

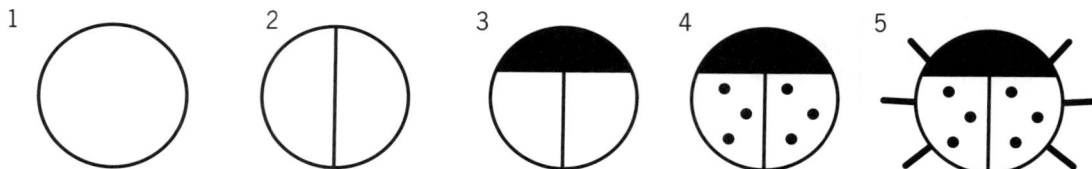

Figure 5.17: The five steps for drawing a ladybird

2   Butterfly: Say *Can you draw a butterfly? Watch me. Draw an oval, like this… Now make two circles on this side… and this side… Here are the antennae: two lines like this… What beautiful butterflies!*

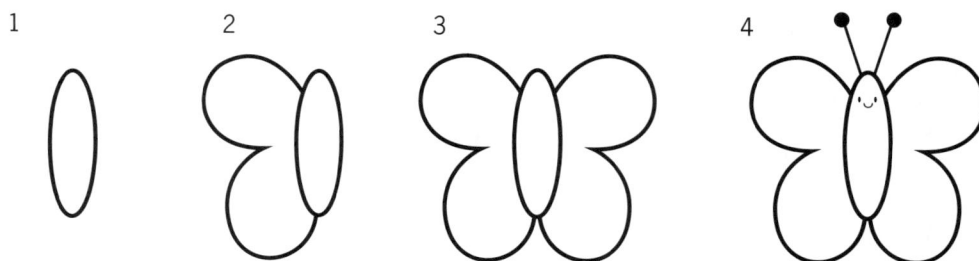

Figure 5.18: The four steps for drawing a butterfly

Extension ideas

•   Once children have mastered the drawings using the steps, they can copy them onto paper and colour or paint their pictures. Turn the pictures into displays; for example, make an *Our insects* display with the ladybirds and butterflies. Add colourful flowers and other insects such as bees, ants and caterpillars.

•   Older children will be able to draw more complex pictures. Look on the internet to find step-by-step instructions for drawing other animals (e.g. cats, dogs and elephants).

•   Use mini-whiteboards to teach children to write numbers. Say the number you are writing on your mini-whiteboard without showing the children until they have attempted their own.

Note

If you are using mini-whiteboards, it's best if the markers are all the same colour (to prevent arguments) and preferably green or blue, to avoid a build-up of dark ink on the boards.

💡 **Tips**

- The use of mini-whiteboards makes this activity appealing because children understand that they're practising. They can rub out mistakes until they're happy with their drawing. Teaching children this skill gives them confidence, since drawing isn't an innate ability but a learned one.

- Drawing shapes and lines to create meaningful symbols helps children to learn to write. It develops their fine motor skills and shows them how to start from the top and work downwards.

5.7 Spring flowers with plasticine

Outline	Children make spring flowers by pressing plasticine onto paper doilies.
Focus	colours, *flower, ball, leaf / leaves, big, small, window*
Age	4–7
Time	20–30 minutes
Materials	A paper doily for each child (or a piece of white paper), plasticine in at least three different colours, green and brown crayons or coloured pencils, sticky tack. Optional: Pictures of flowers.
Preparation	Make some spring flowers to show the class. With younger children, roll the plasticine into balls of differing sizes before you start.

Procedure

1 Show pictures of flowers or draw flowers on the board. Ask *What are these? (Flowers.) What colour is this flower? Pink! And this one? That's right, it's blue. And this one? Yellow!*

2 Show the plasticine flowers you have made and ask about the shapes and colours.

3 Demonstrate how to start the flower by rolling a small ball of plasticine and pushing it into the centre of the paper. Say *Watch me everyone. I'm making a very small ball. It's pink. I'm rolling the plasticine in my hands. It's a small ball. Now look. I'm pushing it on my paper.* Push the ball with your fingers very hard until it sticks to the paper.

4 Take another piece of plasticine and make a smaller ball. Stick it inside the other colour. Say *I have another ball of plasticine. What colour is it? That's right, it's blue. I'm making it very, very small. Smaller than the other one. ... Now I'm pushing this on the pink plasticine. Push it in the middle of the big pink circle. Look! It's my first flower.*

5 Show children how to draw the stem and leaves on the flower using crayons. Say *I'm drawing a stem and leaves. What colour is the stem? Are the leaves big or small?* See also the diagram of a flower on page 139.

6 Say *Let's make spring flowers!* Hand out the doilies / paper and plasticine. Monitor, making sure children are pushing the plasticine into the paper hard enough for it to stick. Ask, e.g. *What colour is your ball? What colour is your big flower, Anne?* Once everyone is working on their flowers, distribute the crayons. Say, e.g. *What big leaves, Susanne. I like your bee, Jack!*

7 Use sticky tack to display the spring flowers. If you stick them on a window, where the children have applied the plasticine thinly enough, the light will shine through.

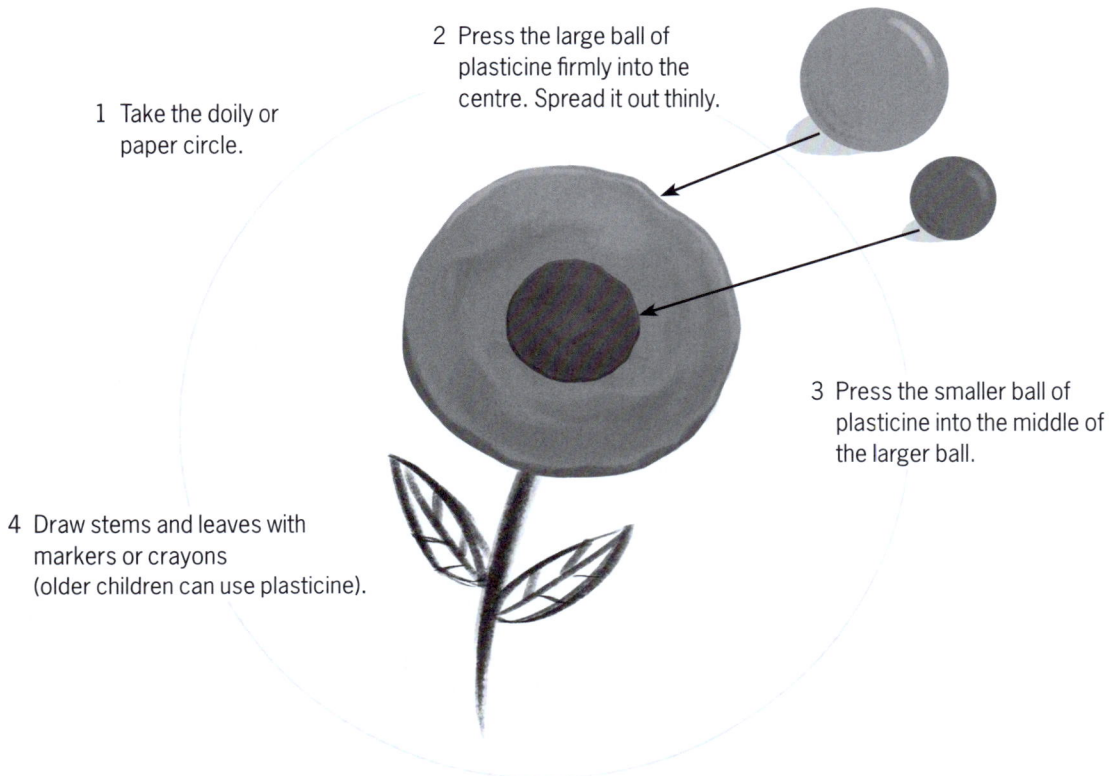

2 Press the large ball of plasticine firmly into the centre. Spread it out thinly.

1 Take the doily or paper circle.

3 Press the smaller ball of plasticine into the middle of the larger ball.

4 Draw stems and leaves with markers or crayons (older children can use plasticine).

Figure 5.19: Making a spring flower with plasticine

Extension ideas

- Use this technique to make different pictures. The flowers are a good starting point because they are easy and help children to understand how to press the plasticine into the paper so that it sticks.
- Children make the flowers on a folded piece of card to create a spring or Mother's Day card.

Note

We learned this activity from artist and inspirational teacher Edith Hatton.

5.8 Salt dough pendants

Outline	Children make pendants in different shapes from salt dough.
Focus	Colours, *roll, star, heart, circle, hole, glue, glitter pendant*
Age	4–7
Time	20–30 minutes over three lessons. The dough takes some time to dry, unless you have access to an oven.
Materials	Lesson 1: A ball of salt dough, two pieces of waxed paper, a paper plate and a straw for each child, rolling pins, cookie cutters.
	Lesson 2: Paints, paintbrushes, cotton buds.
	Lesson 3: Glue, brushes, glitter in shakers, string or thin ribbon (one length for each pendant).
Preparation	Prepare the salt dough. To make 36 (4cm x 4cm) pendants you will need: two cups plain flour, one cup salt, ¾ cup lukewarm water, a mixing bowl and spoon. Mix the flour and salt in the bowl. Add the water slowly, mixing well until you have a dough that holds together. If it sticks to your hands, it's too wet: add some more flour and salt and knead well.
	If possible, make some example pendants to show the class.

Procedure

Lesson 1

1 Show some example pendants. Say *Look at my pendant. What shape is it? That's right, it's a star. Let's make some pendants!*

2 Give each child a small paper plate. Children write their name on their plate (they will put their shapes on the plate to dry).

3 Place a ball of salt dough between pieces of waxed paper and show children how to roll it out. Say *Look, I'm rolling the dough. It's getting flatter and bigger.* If possible, give each child a turn with the rolling pin.

4 Demonstrate cutting some shapes from the dough. Say *Watch me everyone. What's this? … That's right, it's a star. Press like this. Can you do it? Take a cutter and cut a shape. Put it on your plate.* Children cut three shapes each out of the dough.

Figure 5.20: Dough shapes and cutters

5   Show the children how to make holes in the shapes using the straw. Say *Watch, everyone. Here's my straw. Push the straw into the shape to make a hole, here at the top.* Hand out the straws. Children make the holes. Circulate and help.

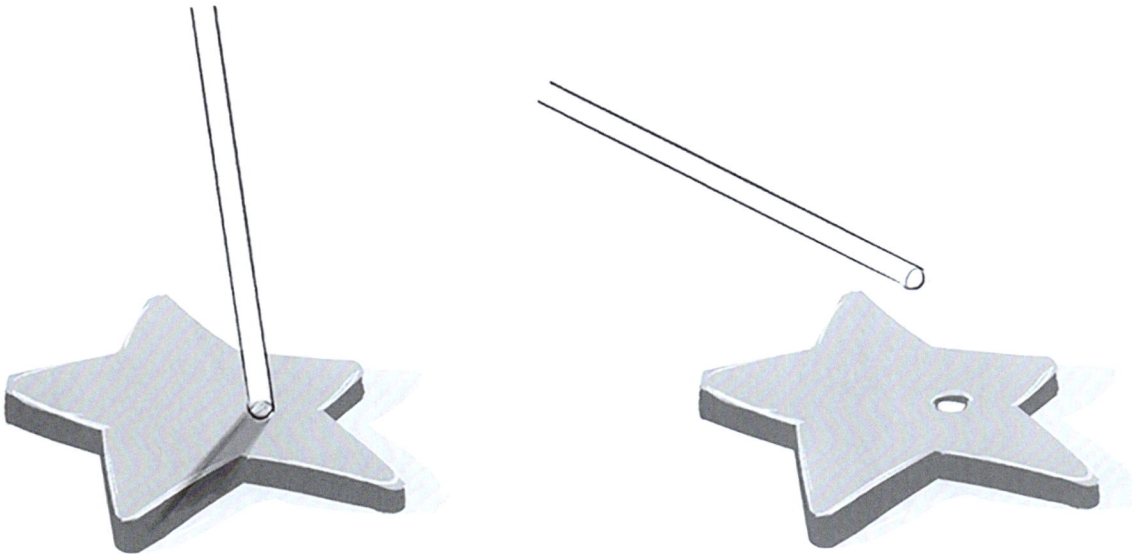

Figure 5.21: Making a hole in a shape using a straw

6   Put the plates in a safe place for the shapes to dry.

Lesson 2
1   Show children how to put a cotton bud in the hole in each shape to keep it steady while they paint.
2   Children paint one side of their shapes. Provide a limited number of colours. Put red paint with brushes on one table, blue paint on another and yellow on another. Children take their plate of shapes to each table, using the brushes for that colour. Show children what they are going to do before they start. Say *Watch me, everyone. Put this cotton bud here, in the hole, like this. Now paint the shape. This table has blue, this table has yellow and this table has red. Paint one shape only. Now watch me. I leave my brush in the water here.* Move to another table and paint another shape.
3   If you have time, children can also paint the other side of the pendants when they are dry.

Lesson 3
1   Children spread white glue on one side of the shapes and sprinkle them with glitter.
2   When the pendants are dry, double a long piece of string or thin ribbon and put it through the hole, slipping the ends through the loop. Tie a knot at the end.

Figure 5.22: Some finished pendants

Variation
With a small class of older children, make the salt dough together in Lesson 1.

Extension ideas
- Make decorations for festivals using the same process. For Christmas decorations, add fine white glitter with white glue to represent snow.
- Make medals. Use only circular cookie cutters. Children press a star stamp design into the centre of each shape. They write their names on the back with felt-tip pens. Cover with gold and silver glitter on one side only. Use the medals in an award ceremony.

Notes
- This activity takes time but it is exciting for the children, who are delighted with the results. The ingredients for salt dough are very cheap compared to shop-bought clays.
- Many things can be made with salt dough, including miniature food and animals, but making shapes using cookie cutters is the easiest for very young children.
- Salt dough can take a long time to air dry. You may need a week between making the shapes and painting them. The shapes can also be dried in an oven on low heat for around four hours. They will last forever if they are painted with white glue or varnish.

5.9 In the ocean 3D display

Outline	Children make a 3D ocean display with moving fish.
Focus	Colours, shapes, *fish, big, small, round, eyes, mouth, tail, stripes, spots, Point to …, How many (red) fish?*
Age	4–7
Time	20–30 minutes
Materials	A piece of A4 coloured card for each child (you will need a selection of colours), crayons, stickers, googly eyes, scissors, hole-punch, a ball of blue yarn, sticky tack.
	Optional: Fish template from the website, a story or video about fish.
Preparation	Make a fish to show the class (a simple oval body and a triangular tail, around the size of an A4 piece of card).

Procedure

1   Read a story about fish or show a video of colourful fish in the ocean.

2   Show the children your fish. Say *Look at my fish. Is it big or small? It's big. Can you draw a big fish?* Draw a fish on the board using an oval for the body and a triangle for the tail. Say *Like this. A big fish. Here's the body and here's the tail.*

3   Give out the card and crayons. Ask *What colour fish are you going to make, Rita? A pink one? Great!* Children draw their fish using the oval and triangle to help them get the shape right.

4   Children write their names on their fish (help younger children with the writing) then they cut them out. Early finishers can start decorating their fish. Comment on the colours and patterns the children use, e.g. *They're nice stripes, Jon. What nice big spots, Carmen! Colour the other side, too.* Hand out stickers, if available. Ask, e.g. *What colour stickers do you want? What shapes?*

5   Give out googly eyes, if you have them, or circles of card. The children stick the eyes on their fish. Say, e.g. *Now the eyes. Yes one on each side, Theo. Oh! You're making a flat fish… the eyes are on the same side!*

6   Collect the fish and, before the next class, make a hole in each one at the top with the hole-punch. Cut pieces of yarn to different lengths and tie a piece to each fish. Attach them to the ceiling with sticky tack a little higher than children can reach.

7   When children come into the room and see the fish hanging from the ceiling, they will be amazed. Play a finding game. Say, e.g. *Point to a red fish. How many blue fish are there? Three! Point to the big fish. Which is the big fish? The green one? That's Telmo's! Can you find some small fish?*

Figure 5.23: Two fish from an In the ocean 3D display

Extension ideas
- Before they take the fish home, have some fun by letting the children hold the fish and make them 'swim' around the room.
- With older children, talk about the problem of pollution in our seas and oceans.

5.10 A handprint tree with butterflies

Outline	Children make a giant tree display with their handprints as the leaves.
Focus	*tree, green, leaf, hand, butterfly, wing, heart, peg*
Age	4–7
Time	20–30 minutes over two or three lessons
Materials	Lesson 1: Brown card to make the tree trunk, white paper (one piece for each handprint), green finger paint, plastic plates. Lesson 2: Scissors, glue sticks. Lesson 3: A wooden peg for each child and different coloured crepe or tissue paper, felt tips, heart and flower shapes cut from coloured paper, glue and crayons.
Preparation	Make a tree trunk with branches from brown card, large enough for a classroom display. Make a leaf from your handprint and a butterfly to show the class (see pictures below). Cut the tissue paper for the butterflies' wings into smallish rectangles (about 15cm x 8cm). Cut out flowers shapes in different sizes and paper hearts from coloured paper.

Procedure

Lesson 1

1 Show children the tree trunk display and ask *What is it? … It's a tree! But it hasn't got leaves. Let's make leaves for our tree.*

2 Demonstrate how to make a handprint on paper using the green paint. Say *Put one hand in the paint, like this. Now put it on the paper, like this.*

3 Hand out plastic plates with paint and pieces of paper. Make as many handprints as you need, depending on the size of your tree (each child can make at least two). Leave them to dry.

Lesson 2

1 Show children how to cut out their handprint(s). If necessary, draw dotted lines with a pencil around the handprints as a guide for cutting.

2 If they can reach, children glue the leaves on the tree display. Otherwise, do this before the next lesson. Don't glue the leaves down completely: leave parts free so that the peg butterflies can be attached.

Lesson 3

1 Show your butterfly to the class and peg it to one of the leaves on the tree.

2 Give out the wooden pegs and felt tips. Children colour the pegs and draw stripes or circles, as they wish. Say, e.g. *What colour is your butterfly, Handa? That's nice – red and blue stripes!*

3 Give out the coloured tissue paper rectangles for the wings (two pieces for each child). Ask, e.g. *What colours do you want? Blue and pink? That will make beautiful wings, Ana!*

4 Show children how to lay the smaller piece of coloured tissue paper over the larger one. Scrunch the paper in the middle and put it between the two parts of the peg. Say, e.g. *Look. Here's my orange paper and here's my pink paper. I'm putting the pink paper on top of the orange paper. Now I'm squeezing it in the middle. Then I'm putting the peg on it, in the middle. … That's right! Well done! What beautiful butterfly wings! What colour are they? Orange and pink!*

5 Children make their butterflies and peg them to the leaves and trunk of the tree.

6 Children glue flowers and paper hearts around the tree. Talk about the finished display, e.g. *I like flowers… and butterflies. Where's your butterfly, Mohan? What colour is it? Can you find the white flower, Judit?*

Figure 5.24: A handprint tree

Figure 5.25: Butterflies made from tissue paper and pegs

Variation
Three year-olds can make handprint leaves but you will need to cut them out.

Extension ideas
* Add a *Thank you, Mother Nature* title to your display. Older children could stick photos of birds and animals that live in trees to the display. They could also add more collage elements (e.g. real leaves, branches and bark rubbings).
* Add other insects (caterpillars, bees, beetles) made from plasticine, stickers or other materials.

- Talk about how important trees are (e.g. they give us oxygen and help clean the air). Bring in real leaves, nuts and fruit to show what trees give us. Talk about things we make from wood (tables, chairs, paper). Plant a real tree at school, if possible.
- If you have a playground with trees, take the children out to look at them. Get them to touch the trees and feel how the bark and leaves are different. Ask *Can you see any fruit, nuts or flowers on the trees? What about insects or birds?*
- Learn about protecting nature and the planet. Make recycling bins for the classroom. (see 6.11 *Recycling bins: paper and plastic* on page 167).

6 Exploring the World

Learning a new language in a classroom where the learners' own language is the same (or at least where several of the children speak the same language) can be a rather artificial process. Sometimes it feels as if it would be so much easier for the children to communicate with each other and with the teacher in their own language.

There are various ways in which the teacher can turn this artificial situation into a more natural one. First of all, by using the new language as a medium of communication rather than a system of words, structures and sounds that needs to be formally taught. Secondly, through drawing on the children's rich imagination; when the teacher tells an intriguing story, for example. Through children's imagination, the story becomes a reality, and the new language itself is part of that reality.

In the very young child's perception of the world, there are no clear lines that separate imagination from reality. Gradually, children begin to explore the world around them and to use their cognitive resources to help them build a coherent model of the world and understand how it works. So the third way of getting children to treat the new language as a natural and meaningful method of interacting with the world and the people around them is by engaging them in real world experiences. Through these experiences children learn to remember, organize and retrieve information about the world around them, and develop their ability to solve problems.

The activities in this chapter help children explore the real world by activating their sensory systems (when they focus on colours, the properties of objects, materials, textures, tastes and smells). Then they are encouraged to think about their experiences and draw conclusions. For example, the teacher engages the learners in an experiment that gets them to think about whether an object will sink or float on water (6.2 *Does it float or sink?*). Then they can test their hypotheses by putting objects in a container filled with water to see if they were right. Such learning episodes offer ideal opportunities for the teacher to use English naturally, and to scaffold the children's language development in such a way that the new language becomes as real as the experiment the children are engaged in.

6.1 Colour magic: mixing colours

Outline	Children mix coloured water to learn how the primary colours combine to make the secondary colours.
Focus	*red, yellow, blue, orange, green, purple, brown, water, mix, What colour is it? What colour do they make? What colour are you making?*
Age	4–7
Time	20–30 minutes
Materials	Three clear plastic bottles with lids and a large plastic bowl for each group of three to four children; a clear plastic cup for each child, water, red, yellow and blue liquid food colouring, rags / paper towels to clean up. Optional: A torch (see *Extension ideas*).
Preparation	Fill the plastic bottles with water. Add several drops of food colouring to the three bottles for each group to make a red bottle, a yellow bottle and a blue bottle, or get the children to do that for you if you are working with six and seven year-olds. Replace the lids. Note: Don't make the colours too dark, but you may need to make the yellow a little stronger than the others. Prepare a set of three bottles for yourself (with colouring) and have a clear plastic cup ready to demonstrate the activity.

Procedure

1   Review colours *red, blue, yellow, orange, green* and *purple*. Hold up the three bottles of coloured water in turn and ask *What colour is this? That's right! It's red / yellow / blue.*

2   Say *Today we're going to do an experiment.* Ask *What happens when we mix colours? Let's mix colours.* Mime mixing. Take the tops off the red and yellow water bottles. Place a clear plastic cup between them. First, pour the yellow water in the cup. Say *What colour is it?* Hold up the red bottle and ask *What colour is it?* Say *Let's mix the colours!* Then add red water to the cup until you get orange. Hold up the cup and ask *What colour is it? … That's right, it's orange!*

3   Distribute three bottles of coloured water to each group and give a plastic cup to each child. Put a plastic bowl on each table for children to pour their finished liquids into. Place paper and absorbent rags at each table to catch spills.

4   In their groups, children take turns mixing yellow and red (to make orange), yellow and blue (to make green) and blue and red (to make purple). As they work ask, e.g. *What colour do they make? What colour are you making, Jon? Green? You've got blue and what other colour? Yellow?*

5   After a child has made each new colour, they tip the water from the cup into the bowl on their table, so that they can make a different colour in their cup.

6   At the end of the activity, you will have bowls of dark-coloured water on each table. This will delight the children! Say *Look, brown / black / grey!*

Variation

With very large classes you may have to do the experiment as a whole group. Involve the children by asking them what colours they want to make and getting volunteers to help mix the colours for you. Use six bottles with tops you can close. Children pass the colours around once they're made.

Extension ideas

- Show six bottles with different coloured water at the front of the class and ask children to help you put them in the order of the colours in a rainbow. Show a picture of a rainbow to help. Children say *Yes* or *No* as you put the bottles in different orders.
- The colours can be very beautiful. Your children will be delighted if you turn the lights down and shine a torch through the plastic bottles. If you have a whiteboard, the reflected patterns are lovely.
- Sing a rainbow song with the class while pointing to the colours, for example, *It's red and yellow, pink and green / It's purple, orange and blue / It's a lovely rainbow / And it's for you!*
- Display the bottles, labelled with the colours, on a classroom shelf and use them instead of flashcards when you want to revise the colours.
- On a sunny day, hand out old CDs to the children, one per pair. Ask them to go to a window and to move the CD gently, look at it carefully and say what they can see (a rainbow). They say the colours in their pairs.

Note

We learned the last extension idea from Peter Lewis-Jones, Herbert's co-author on *Super Safari*, (Cambridge University Press, 2015).

6.2 Does it float or sink?

Outline	Children experiment to see if different objects float or sink in water.
Focus	*Does it float / sink? yes, no, It floats. It sinks. tick, cross*
Age	4–6
Time	20–30 minutes
Materials	A plastic tub filled with water or a water tray for each small group of children. A variety of eight objects which float or sink in water (e.g. objects that float: pegs, plastic objects (boats, rubber ducks, empty bottles), pieces of light wood, cork, leaves, apples; objects that sink: metal paper clips, coins, keys, glass marbles, stones, carrots) Optional: *Does it float or sink?* worksheet (see page 153 or the website).
Preparation	Fill the trays / bowls with water. Optional: Photocopy a *Does it float or sink?* worksheet for each child (see page 153). If using different objects you will need to modify the worksheet.

Procedure

1   Demonstrate the activity. Draw two of the objects you are going to use in the experiment on the board, one that floats and one that doesn't (for example a key and a ball). Draw a tick box next to each picture on the board.

2   Hold up the object that will sink in water and say *Look! It's a (key). I'm going to put it in the water.* Use mime to show what you are going to do. Ask *What's going to happen? Float or sink?* Use mime to show the meaning of the two words.

3   Put the object in the water. Ask *Does it float?* Mime ticking. *Or does it sink?* Mime making a cross. Put a cross in the box next to the picture on the board. Say *It sinks.* Repeat for the object that floats (e.g. a plastic ball). This time put a tick in the box next to your picture and say *It floats.*

4   Get children to predict before they do the experiment themselves. Hold up each item and ask *Does it float? Does it sink?* Encourage children to say *It floats* or *It sinks.*

5   In groups, children experiment by putting different objects in the water. Circulate and say e.g. *It's your turn Maria. What are you going to try? The boat? OK! What do you think, Anna? Will it float or sink? Sink? Let's see! Does it float?*

6   Give out the worksheets and pencils. Children experiment and then tick or cross the items. Say, e.g. *Let's see! Does it float? Yes! Can you put a tick in the box? Well done!*

7   At the end of the activity, hold up each item and ask *Does it float or sink?* Encourage children to say *It floats* or *It sinks.*

Variations

1   If doing this experiment as a whole class, make sure that each child gets to put an object in the water. Before they put it in the water, ask *What do you think? Will it float or sink?*

2   If you have a playground, you could do this experiment outdoors. Place a bowl of water on the ground. Children collect objects and bring them to you. Ask *Will it float or sink?* before they place each object in the water.

Extension idea

With older children, watch a short video about boats. Ask children to say whether the boats are big or small as they watch. Explain that the shape helps them to float: *See the bottom of the boat* (gesture with your hands to make the shape of the hull). *It's like a cup.* Put a small metal or ceramic bowl in water to show how it floats.

	Float	Sink

6.3 Magnet magic

Outline	Children explore the phenomenon of magnetism.
Focus	*magnet, The (paper clip) is magnetic. The (paper) is not magnetic. Is it magnetic? Move it close to the magnet. You're right / wrong.*
Age	5–7
Time	15–20 minutes
Materials	One magnet per group of three to four children, a paper clip, a small metal ball (e.g. a ball bearing), a pencil, plastic, paper, plus other small objects (some of which are attracted to magnets, some not). Optional: Four wooden blocks, a wooden or plastic kitchen tray and some sand, coloured if possible (see *Extension ideas*).
Preparation	Practise demonstrating magnetism with the objects.

Procedure

1   Show the children a magnet. Say *It's a magnet.* Take a paper clip and say *Look, it's a paper clip. A paper clip.* Get the children to repeat each of the words *magnet* and *paper clip* several times.

2   Ask a child to take the magnet. Ask another child to take the paper clip. Say, *(Lisa), move the paper clip closer to the magnet.* Show them what you mean. Say *Look. It's magnetic. The paper clip's magnetic.* Get the children to repeat the word after you several times. Once children have discovered that some things can be attracted to a magnet they are usually fascinated and want to try this again and again.

3   Ask a different child to take the magnet, and another to hold a different magnetic object (e.g. an iron key). Ask *Is it magnetic?* The child with the object moves it closer to the magnet to find out. Say *Yes, it is. The paper clip is magnetic and the key is magnetic.*

4   Give the magnet to a different child and hand another child the piece of paper. Show him / her how to crumple the paper into a ball. Say *Make a ball. Move it closer to the magnet.* Most children will expect the paper ball to show the same effect as the two objects before, and will be surprised there is no magnetic attraction this time. Say *The paper is not magnetic. The paper clip **is** magnetic. The key **is** magnetic. The paper is **not** magnetic.*

5   Get the children to find out whether each of the other objects is magnetic or not. Divide the class into groups of three to four and give each group a magnet. Comment on what the children are doing and discovering as they work, e.g. *Is it magnetic? What do you think? Move it close to the magnet. You're right / wrong!*

Extension idea

Put wooden blocks beneath a tray, one at each corner, to raise the tray about 15 cm above the table. Ask a child to put the paper clip onto the tray. Get them to hold the magnet underneath the tray, and move it to the spot where the paper clip is lying. Once they can see that the paper clip gets drawn to the magnet, comment on what you can see, e.g. *Wow! Look. The paper clip is magnetic. Now move the magnet* (make a gesture as if moving an imaginary paperclip with the fingers of your hand). *Look. The paper clip is moving too. Wow! It's magnetic. It's moving.* Let other children repeat the same experiment, and use other objects (magnetic and non-magnetic ones).

Spread a thin layer of sand across the tray, then ask a child to move the paper clip by moving a magnet in a circle below it, saying *Hold the magnet like this. Now make a circle. ... Look at the sand. What can you see in the sand? ... Yes, it's a circle.*

6.4 Big or small?

Outline	Children explore the concepts *big* and *small*.
Focus	*What's this? Is it big or small? It's (big / small). What have you got? A big / small (car).* Revision of known words, e.g. *car, boat, train, bus*
Age	4–6
Time	10–15 minutes
Materials	Toys / models of small and big items (e.g. a small toy car, a big toy car, a small toy boat, a big toy boat, a small train and a big train, a small bus and a big bus), a piece of A4 paper per child, crayons. Optional: A blindfold. Extension idea: Poster paper and a glue stick.
Preparation	None

Procedure

1 Show the children a big toy car and a small toy car. Say *Look. I've got two cars. Two cars.* Point at the cars. Get children to repeat *Two cars.* Revise colours if you wish by saying *Point at the (green) car. Point at the (red) car.* Then say *Look. The (green) car is small. It's small.* Make a gesture with the fingers of one hand indicating *small.* Then say *The (red) car is big. It's big. Big.* Make a gesture with both hands, indicating *big.* Repeat with the other toys.

2 Get the children to sit in a circle. Put all the toys on the floor in the middle. Call a child by name and say *Give me the small boat, please.* Encourage the child to say *Here you are* when they give you the right toy, and say *Thank you.* If the child offers you the wrong toy, repeat your request and help by gently pointing at the right toy. Continue until several children have had a turn.

3 Put a chair next to you. Ask a child to sit in the chair and close their eyes (or blindfold the child). Ask him / her to hold out both hands. Place a small toy in the child's left hand and a big toy in the child's right hand. Ask *What is it?* The child will probably just say something like *bus.* Say, e.g. *That's right. You've got two buses. A small bus and a big bus. Hold up the small bus, please. And now hold up the big bus.* The child holds up the correct toy each time. Continue until several children have had a turn.

Extension ideas

• Make a *Big and Small* poster with older children. Collect pictures of big and small objects, for example, pictures of adult and children's shoes, big and small boats, elephants as opposed to insects. Catalogues and magazines are good sources of pictures. Alternatively, give the materials to the children and ask them to cut out pictures of big and small things. Check the pictures and say, e.g. *Let's see what you've got here. Ah, that's nice. A big house and a small one. Let's stick them on the poster. Can you stick the big house on the poster, please? Thanks. And now take the small house and stick it on.*

• Teach a chant or song about opposites, for example, 2.4 *Opposites actions* (see page 58).

6.5 Rubbings: surfaces and textures

Outline	Children explore different surfaces and textures by making rubbings.
Focus	*crayon, paper, rub, gently,* general vocabulary, e.g. *leaf, tree, coin, basket*
Age	3–7
Time	10–15 minutes
Materials	Paper and a crayon for each child, a selection of interesting objects / surfaces for the rubbings (e.g. coins, leaves, leather items, plastic and wicker bags / baskets, woven fabric, bark from trees, buttons, embroidery and beaded surfaces).
Preparation	If your children are doing this activity indoors, put around six objects on each table (see list above). If your children are doing the activity outdoors, look around for examples of textures children could use (but they will choose things themselves). Make some example rubbings of different surfaces.

Procedure

1 Show the children your paper with rubbings. Say, e.g. *Look at my paper. There are four things here. What's this? Yes, it's a leaf. Now watch me.* Put a piece of paper on top of a textured surface, such as a wall or a basket. Rub carefully over it using a crayon to bring out the surface pattern.

2 Give a piece of paper and a crayon to each child and ask or help them to write their names.

3 If children are doing this activity in the classroom, they choose four or more items from their table and do a rubbing of each one with their crayon. Circulate and say, e.g. *What do you want to rub? What about this coin? Well done, Tim! The coin looks beautiful!*

4 If children are doing the activity in the playground, they can use anything they can find to do the rubbings. Help by suggesting objects / surfaces, until the children are confident to find things on their own, e.g. *That leaf looks good. Look at that tree, Jessie. Can you rub this part? What does it feel like? Is it rough or smooth?*

5 Set a time limit or a limit on the number of objects. Show individual efforts to the class. Say, e.g. *Who's finished? Show us what you have done. Wow! Look at this. Well done, Sarah. What has Sarah got? Yes, it's a leaf!* If the rubbings have been done with objects in the classroom, ask the child to hold up or go to the object that they rubbed to make the pattern.

Figure 6.1: Examples of rubbings

Variations
1 Use just one type of object for the rubbings, such as leaves or coins. Children rub the leaves / coins and then cut them out. See if they can match other children's cut-outs with the original item. Use the rubbings to make a display.
2 If you have a playground with lots of different kinds of trees, get children to do rubbings of all the tree trunks. Some bark is rough and some is smooth. Get children to feel the bark before they rub it. Ask *Is it rough or smooth?* Collect different leaves to match to the tree trunk rubbings.

6.6 Planting seeds

Outline	Children plant seeds and watch them grow to learn what a plant needs to survive.
Focus	*cup, seed, soil, water, air, sun, grow, plant, leaves*
Age	3–7
Time	30 minutes (and time for the plant to grow)
Materials	A plastic cup or yoghurt pot for each child, seeds (radish seeds are the easiest to grow, but you could also use nasturtium, zinnia, cosmos, marigold, pumpkin or melon seeds), paper plates, soil in a plastic tub and water in a plastic bottle for each group, large tray, stickers.
Preparation	Prepare a pot, soil and seed to demonstrate the activity to the class.

Procedure

1   Show a short video of a plant growing, read about plants and what they need or tell the story *The Enormous Turnip* (see page 110).

2   Use the video or story and draw pictures to teach the words children will need for the activity: *seed, soil, water, air, sun, grow, plant, leaves.*

3   Demonstrate the activity. Hold up a cup, fill it with soil and put the seeds in, then water the seeds. Talk as you show the children what to do, e.g. *Here's my cup. I'm putting soil in the cup … carefully! What's this? Yes, it's a tiny seed. It grows into a plant. I'm going to put ten seeds in my soil. Let's count them… one, two, three… I'm pushing the seeds down, but not too far. Like this, this far* (show the tip of your finger). *Now I'm putting in the water … not too much! Not too much water or my plant will not grow.*

4   Children plant their seeds step by step. First distribute the plastic cups / pots. Then put the containers of soil with cups or spoons in the centre of each table. Say *Put the soil in the cups.* Circulate and help / comment, e.g. *Like this… . Take turns. Who's first? Simon? OK. Then you, Julia. Be careful! Very good!*

5   Once the children have put the soil in their cups, give out the seeds by putting some on a paper plate on each table. Say *Put the seeds in the soil now. Remember, ten seeds only. Count! One, two, three… .* Circulate and help / comment, as before, e.g. *Put the seeds in the soil gently. Push just a little bit.*

6   Hand out the plastic bottles of water. Say *Now put the water in the cups. A little! Not too much.* Children take turns to water their seeds. It's important that they understand that too much water is not good for plants.

7   Hand out the stickers and pencils. Children write their names on the stickers and stick them on their pots. With younger children, write the names yourself. Put the pots in trays near a window, for example, on the windowsill. Talk about what the plants need to grow: soil, water, air and sun. Children will excitedly watch for the first signs that their plants are growing!

8   In circle time have a 'plant watching' spot, getting a child to look for signs of growth and to check the soil to see if it needs watering. A spray bottle is good for this. When the young plants are strong enough, each child can take theirs home. Tell the children to plant it outside, if they have a garden, balcony or window box.

Extension ideas

- Do a theatre activity. Two children play the role of farmers. The rest of the class will be the seeds. They all sit on the floor. One of the 'farmers' walks around touching the children on their heads gently. These children curl up into ball shapes. This is 'planting' the seeds. Pretend to be a seed yourself. Then the other 'farmer' walks around and 'waters' the curled-up children (with an empty cup or, culture permitting, a spray bottle with a little bit of water in it). Lead the activity by starting to 'grow'. Slowly uncurl yourself, stand up gradually and reach upwards. The children on the floor do the same, pretending to become strong plants, their arms outstretched.
- As their plants grow, older children can make a labelled drawing or collage showing the parts of the plant.
- Talk about seeds as food: ask *What animals eat seeds?* Put seeds out for the birds if you have an outside area at school.

6.7 What does it taste like?

Outline	Children use their sense of taste to identify different foods. They practise answering the question *What does it taste like?*
Focus	Food, *I (don't) like … What does it taste like? It's / It tastes good / nice / fantastic / yummy / horrible. What is it? It's (carrot).*
Age	6–7
Time	10–15 minutes
Materials	Different foods which can be eaten raw (e.g. apples, ice cream, chocolate, carrots, bread, biscuits), a blindfold. Optional: A raw onion (see *Extension idea*).
Preparation	Cut the foods into bitesize pieces.
Important note:	Do not use foods which are too small, such as sweets, as children could choke. Never use nuts. Check with parents that there are no children with allergies to the foods you are using.

Procedure

1   The children sit around a table or in a circle on the floor. Put the food on a big plate in the middle. Present / review the words for the food you have brought.

2   Say one of the words. Get the children to point at the correct food.

3   Point at one of the foods, and say, e.g. *I like (apples). What about you, (Carlos)?* Get the children to take turns pointing and saying *I like … / I don't like …*.

4   Put several pieces of each food on a plate. Offer the plate to a child and say *Choose one piece. What would you like?* When a child has taken something say, *Ah, you've chosen the (apple). Do you like (apples)?* Prompt the child to say *Yes, I do. I like (apples).*

5   Say *Taste it. What does it taste like? Is it nice?* Prompt the child to say *It tastes nice* or *It's nice.* Repeat with different children and teach different phrases for talking about food, e.g. *It's / It tastes fantastic / yummy / horrible.*

6   Blindfold one of the children. Ask the other children to select pieces of three different foods and put them on a plate. The children offer the plate to the child with the blindfold. Say *Pick it up … Open your mouth. Now taste it. What is it? / What does it taste like?* Prompt / help the child to say *It's (carrot). / It tastes (nice).*

7   Repeat with children taking turns to wear the blindfold. Gradually, get the children to use more and more of the language themselves, but be ready to prompt if necessary.

Variation

Use pictures / flashcards instead of real food – children pretend to taste it.

Extension idea

Once children are familiar with the game, hold a freshly cut onion for the blindfolded child to smell (but not to touch or taste!). They try tasting the foods straight after smelling the onion. Children are often rather surprised that because of the strong smell of the onion, they find it difficult or impossible to name the foods they are tasting.

6.8 Fruit and vegetables

Outline	Children find out about fruit and vegetables and practise categorizing.
Focus	Fruit and vegetables, e.g. *apples, carrots, strawberries, bananas, carrots, potatoes, broccoli; Is it a fruit or a vegetable? (It's a) fruit / vegetable.*
	Extension idea: *Let's wash the (apple) first. Let's cut it up. Put it in the bowl. Stir it. Let's add some orange juice.* (mainly receptive)
Age	5–7
Time	20–25 minutes
Materials	Various fruits and vegetables or flashcards, e.g. an apple, a carrot, strawberries, a banana, a potato, some broccoli.
	Optional: If you decide to make a real fruit salad: some knives (one sharp, the rest blunt), a chopping board, a big bowl, some orange juice and a large spoon. If you want the children to taste the fruit salad: a bowl and a spoon for each child.
Preparation	Put the fruits and vegetables (or the pictures) on a tray.

Procedure

1 Show the real fruit and vegetables or the flashcards to teach the words. Take different fruit and vegetables from the tray in turn and always put them back in a different place.

2 Name one of the fruits or vegetables. The children point at it (or come to the front and pick it up).

3 Pick up one of the fruits, for example, an apple (or use the flashcard). Say *An apple is a fruit. A fruit. A fruit.* The children repeat the word. Then put the apple on the table, on one side of the tray. Pick up one of the vegetables, for example, a carrot. Say *A carrot is a vegetable. A vegetable. A vegetable.* The children repeat the word. Then put the carrot on the table, on the other side of the tray.

4 Ask a child to come to the front and say, e.g. *Take a potato.* Wait for the child to pick up the right item, then ask *Fruit or vegetable?* If necessary, help the child to put it on the appropriate side of the tray (next to the other vegetable).

5 Continue in this way with the other fruits and vegetables or flashcards.

6 Get the children to put everything back on the tray in random order, and repeat the categorization activity (from step 3).

Extension ideas

• If you're using flashcards, draw a big bowl on the board. Tell the children that you are going to make a fruit salad (draw some fruit in the bowl to help explain the meaning). Put all the fruit and vegetable pictures in random order face down in front of you.

Get a child to pick one, and hold it up so everyone can see it clearly. Ask the children to name the item. Ask *Can we put it in the fruit salad?* The children answer *Yes* or *No*, depending on whether the picture is a fruit or a vegetable.

If the picture is a piece of fruit, say *Let's cut it up.* Invite the children to use an imaginary knife to mime cutting the fruit. Then say *Let's put it into the bowl.* Children mime putting the pieces into a bowl.

Continue in this way with all the other flashcards. When all the fruit is in the imaginary bowl, say *Let's add some orange juice.* Mime pouring in the juice. The children copy you. Say *And now let's stir it.* Mime stirring, with the children copying, as before.

Mime serving the fruit salad, if you wish. Ask individual children, e.g. *Some fruit salad, (Emily)?* Prompt the children to say *Yes* or *No*. Mime putting some fruit salad into an imaginary bowl and giving it to the children who say *Yes*. Say *Taste it*. Get these children to mime eating with a spoon. Then ask *Is it nice?*

• Make a real fruit salad, if possible. This can be great fun for the children, but requires more time, of course. If you do this, make sure that you cut hard fruit such as apple yourself (for safety reasons), and invite the children to cut soft fruit, such as strawberries or banana, using blunt knives. In any case, make sure no child uses a knife (even a blunt one) without your assistance.

6.9 Kitchen or bathroom?

Outline	Children use their sense of smell to categorize different odours.
Focus	*kitchen, bathroom, What's inside? Smell (it)!*
Age	4–7
Time	10–15 minutes
Materials	Eight to ten small tins with lids or yoghurt pots with aluminium foil on top (it is important that they are not transparent), various non-toxic substances with distinctive smells, around half of which come from the kitchen and half from the bathroom, e.g. lemon juice, vinegar, cinnamon, cheese, coffee, tea, shower gel, shampoo, nail polish, toothpaste, soap, a blindfold.
Preparation	Put a different substance into each tin / pot and close it.

Procedure

1 Teach / revise *kitchen* and *bathroom* using flashcards or simple drawings. Practise the words so that the children can use them confidently.

2 Show the children one of the pots, without removing the lid. Ask *What's inside?* Give the class time to come up with ideas, but do not tell them what's inside the pot. Just listen and make comments, e.g. *Ah, you think there's … in it. Really? Do you think this is big enough for a …?*

3 Blindfold a child. Explain (in the children's own language, if necessary) that you are going to give him / her the pot. The child should hold it carefully, smell it and say where they would find this thing: *kitchen* or *bathroom*.

4 Open a pot, give it to the blindfolded child and say *Smell it! Kitchen or bathroom?* Wait for the child to answer. Then give the pot to a different child who can look inside. Say *What do you think? Kitchen or bathroom?* Confirm, e.g. *You're right. It's from the kitchen. It's coffee.* Or pass the pot to another child to guess.

5 Ask the child to take off the blindfold. Hand him / her the pot and say, e.g. *Look. It's coffee. It's from the kitchen. Smell it.* Give them a bit of time to smell the substance again.

6 Repeat, with a different child wearing the blindfold each time, until you have used all the pots.

Extension idea

Once children are familiar with the game and the words for the different substances, you can make it more challenging. The child with the blindfold has to say the name of the place and also the name of the substance (e.g. *Kitchen! Coffee!*).

6.10 Animal habitats: farm, forest or ocean?

Outline	The children categorize animals according to their habitat.
Focus	Habitats: *farm, forest, ocean*; animals from different habitats, e.g. *dolphin, octopus, shark, tiger, monkey, frog, cow, horse, hen, What's this? Where does it live? Where do they live? In the forest / ocean. On a farm.*
Age	4–7
Time	15–20 minutes
Materials	Pictures of habitats from books, posters or the internet: a forest, a farm and the ocean, pictures or flashcards of animals (three from each habitat), e.g. dolphin, octopus, shark, tiger, monkey, frog, cow, horse, hen. Three pieces of poster paper in light green, dark green and light blue, brown card, crayons, scissors and sticky tack, felt pen, copy of the worksheet for each child.
Preparation	Put the pieces of light green, dark green and light blue poster paper on the wall, next to each other. If possible, stick a picture of a habitat at the top of each part of the poster (light green – farm, dark green – forest, light blue – ocean). Alternatively, write the names of the habitats. Stick some brown card on the dark green part of the poster to make tree trunks (so it looks like a forest). Photocopy the worksheet (see page 166 or the website) so that each child has at least two of the animals to colour and cut out.

Procedure

1 Show the children the picture of a forest. Say *forest* and get the children to repeat the word several times. Repeat with the other habitats.
2 Hold up each animal picture or flashcard and elicit or teach the word. Make a game of it by using gestures (see the first Extension idea, below). With very young children, reduce the number of animals to six (two for each habitat).
3 Once children know the animals, choose one of the pictures and say, e.g. *What's this? … Yes, it's a shark! Farm? Forest? Ocean? … That's right! A shark lives in the ocean.*
4 Give each child at least two animals from the worksheet to colour and cut out.
5 Ask a child to come to the poster with one of their animal pictures (e.g. a cow). Elicit the name of the animal, then point at the poster and ask *Where does it live?* If the child points to or says the correct habitat, say e.g. *That's right. Cows live on farms.* If the child needs support, point at the animal and the three habitats and say, e.g. *Cows… Where do they live? In the forest? On the farm? In the ocean?* Help the child find the correct habitat and give him / her sticky tack to put the picture on the poster.
6 Ask another child to come to the front with a picture and continue in this way until all the animal pictures are stuck on the poster.

Extension ideas

• Teach mimes and sounds for the animals. The children copy. For example, make a wavy movement with your hand to represent the way dolphins swim; wobble and move your limbs in a jelly-like fashion for the octopus; show your teeth to indicate the shark; mime stalking for the tiger; swing your arms as if moving through a tree for the monkey; jump like the frog; use your index fingers to show the horns on the cow; mime galloping for the horse and cluck and move your arms like wings for the hen.

Once the children are familiar with the mimes, say one of the animals, e.g. *Dolphin*. The children do the mime and point to the animal on the poster. Or mime the action and ask children to say the name of the animal.

- Ask children to find pictures of other animals at home, cut them out with the help of their parents and bring them to class. When a child brings a new animal, teach the word and ask the child who has brought the picture to stick it on the poster in the appropriate habitat.
- Revise the animals regularly by pointing at the pictures on the poster and asking the children to say the words. Gradually, encourage the children to say *in the ocean*, *in the forest* and *on the farm*. When they can say these prepositional phrases with ease, tell the children to sit with their backs to the poster, and ask individuals, e.g. *Where do sharks live?* The child answers, e.g. *In the ocean*, then checks by turning round, going to the poster, and pointing at the animal.
- Teach a habitat chant. Line up with the children. Teach the chant below with the actions (in brackets). Speak loudly the first time, getting quieter and quieter. Repeat the habitats until all the animals have been named or everyone has had a turn.

We're walking in the forest, the forest, the forest.	(walk like explorers)
Ssh!	(stop and look around)
What can we see?	(point to a forest animal on the habitats poster or ask a child to say one)
We see a … tiger!	
We're swimming in the ocean, the ocean, the ocean.	(mime swimming)
Ssh!	(stop and look around)
What can we see?	(point to an ocean animal or ask a child)
We see a … shark!	
We're riding on the farm, on the farm, on the farm.	(mime riding a horse)
Ssh!	(stop and look around)
What can we see?	(point to a farm animal or ask a child)
We see a … cow!	

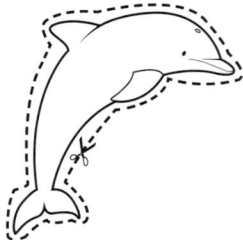

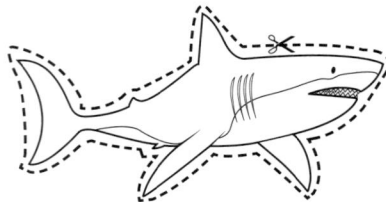

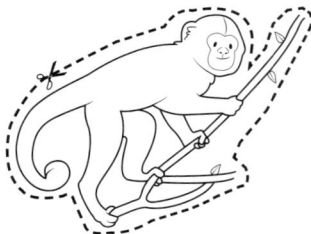
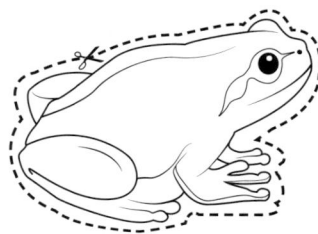
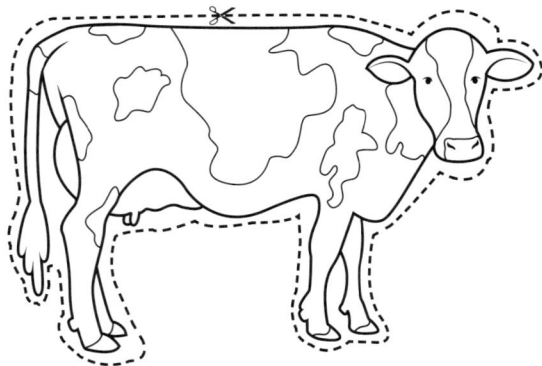

6.11 Recycling bins: paper and plastic

Outline	Children explore materials and learn which ones can be recycled. They make class recycling bins for paper and plastic.
Focus	*paper, plastic, same, different, box, rubbish, recycle, good, bad, clean, dirty*
Age	4–5
Time	15–20 minutes
Materials	Two large boxes or bins, glue, two labels for the recycling bins (see page 168 or the website), used paper, old newspapers, magazines and cardboard items; plastic bottles, containers and bottle tops (enough for each child to put one item in the bin). Optional: Pictures of clean and dirty beaches, parks and forests.
Preparation	Photocopy the labels for the recycling bins (see page 168 or the website).

Procedure

1   Before the class, put some items which can be recycled on the tables, or have a pile of recyclable items ready to show in circle time (e.g. plastic bottles, old newspapers).

2   If possible, show pictures of clean and dirty environments to the children (e.g. a clean beach and a dirty beach). Say, for example, *Look at the two pictures. Can you see the rubbish? The plastic, here? Is this clean or dirty? … Yes, it's dirty. It's bad for animals and people.*

3   Show children an item made of plastic and an item made of paper or card. Say *Are they the same or different? Look. This is plastic and this is paper.* Ask children to find the same materials in the classroom *Can you point to some plastic in the classroom? And some paper?*

4   Show children the two large boxes. While they are watching, glue the two labels on the boxes, and say *Look. This box is for plastic and this box is for paper.* Children take turns to put an item from your pile into one of the boxes. Say, e.g. *Can you find some paper to put in this box, Leo? Amina, can you find some plastic? Good! Put the plastic bottle in the box. No – not that one. Can you see it's for paper?* Make sure to have enough items for all the children to join in.

5   Keep the recycling bins in a specific area and encourage children to use them throughout the year.

Extension ideas

- If you have recycling bins for the whole school, take the children to see them (if possible, taking some of your items to recycle with you). Ask what goes in each bin, e.g. *What goes in the big yellow bin? That's right, it's for plastic. The blue one? Yes, that's for paper. And the green one? That's for glass. Let's put our paper and plastic in the bins!*

- Watch a video about the life cycles of plastic bottles and what happens to them when recycled (they're turned into other plastic things) and when they're not recycled (they break down and fish and other animals eat them, and they die). There are plenty of videos / short animations on the internet.

Note

Sometimes we think that we have to keep every piece of paper a child has written on. In fact, it's good to let go of some of their work. Encourage children to use the bin for their old work, and to keep only things they want to take home or display. Use mini-whiteboards if you can, to save paper.

plastic

paper

PHOTOCOPIABLE

6.12 A weather station

Outline	Children observe the weather and record the changes on an interactive weather station display.
Focus	*What's the weather like today? It's ..., sunny, cloudy, rainy, windy, stormy, snowy;* Extension ideas: *Is it windy today? What's the temperature? cold, cool, mild, warm, hot*
Age	3–7
Time	5 minutes in each class (Note: Children can also use the weather dial(s) whenever they notice the weather changing during a lesson.)
Materials	Two large paper plates, a paper fastener, a photocopy of the weather symbols (see page 171 or the website); Extension ideas: Three paper plates, two paper fasteners, orange, green and blue paint, an arrow made of foam or durable cardboard.
Preparation	Make the *What's the weather like today?* dial from the paper plates and weather symbols (see *Procedure*, steps 1 and 2). You could get groups of children to make a weather dial each, if you have a small class.

Procedure

1 Make the *What's the weather like today?* dial using two paper plates. Cut out and stick the six weather symbols on page 171 (sunny, sunny and cloudy, cloudy, rainy, snowy, stormy) around the edge of one plate, equal distances apart. Alternatively, draw the weather symbols around the plate yourself.

2 Cut an almost triangular section out of the second plate (slightly larger than a weather icon). Write *today It's ... today!* around the edge of this plate and attach it on top of the first plate with a paper fastener. See the photograph below.

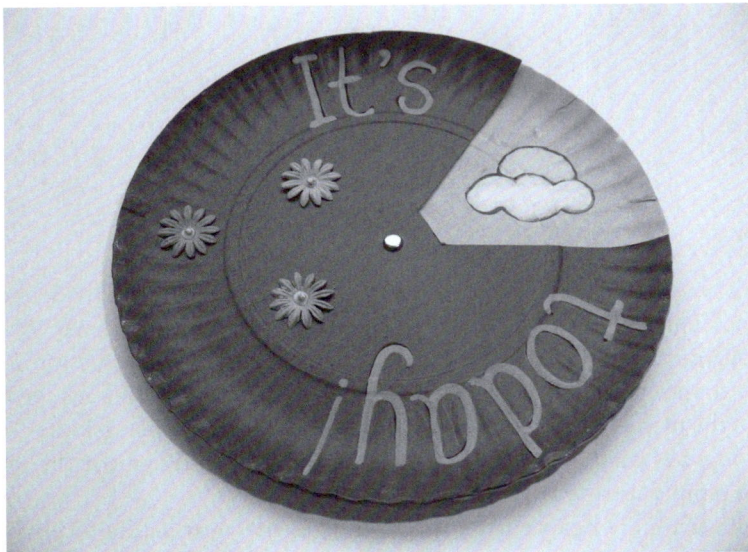

Figure 6.2: A 'What's the weather like today?' dial

3 Fix the dial to your noticeboard or the wall at a height the children can reach.

4 Establish a regular time in class to ask *What's the weather like today?* Ask the children to look out of the window, if possible. Say, e.g. *Sara, can you go to the window and tell us, please? Harry, can you ask Sara: What's the weather like today?* The child says, e.g. *It's cloudy today.* Ask another child to move the dial to the correct symbol (e.g. the clouds).

5 Encourage children to change the dial if they see that the weather has changed during a class.

Extension ideas

• Make a weather station by adding other dials to your display. Make an *Is it windy today?* dial. Divide a paper plate into two halves by drawing a line. Stick the pictures of a tree from page 171 on the plate, the wind-blown tree on one half and the still tree on the other half. Cut a section out of the other plate (large enough to show one of the trees). Attach the second plate on top of the first with a paper fastener. As part of your weather routine, ask *Is it windy today?* and choose a child to move the dial to the correct tree.

Figure 6.3: An 'Is it windy?' dial

• Make a *What's the temperature today?* dial from another paper plate. Divide the plate into thirds by drawing lines. Paint one third blue, one third green and one third orange. Write *cold, cool,* in the blue section, *mild* in the green section and *warm, hot* in the orange section. Attach a cardboard or foam arrow to the centre of the plate with a paper fastener. Write *What's the temperature today?* in the centre of the plate. In each class, after asking about the weather, ask the class *What's the temperature today? Is it cold? Is it hot? Is it mild?* Choose a child to move the arrow to the correct colour and / or temperature word on the dial.

• If you have a playground or garden area, take the class and weather dial(s) outside to create a total weather experience.

• Older children can make their own dial(s) to take home.

• Use your weather dial(s) when singing *It's cold outside* (Activity 3.5, page 75).

From *Activities for Very Young Learners* © Cambridge University Press 2017 PHOTOCOPIABLE

7 Thinking-based activities

It's obvious that nobody knows what tomorrow's world will be like. What's not so clear, however, is the way in which education can equip children with the skills they need to be successful in their future lives. How can we prepare them if we do not know exactly what kind of world they will be living in?

The answer is for us to help our students to go beyond the acquisition of factual knowledge. They need to learn to assess new information, understand unexpected situations, make decisions and evaluate whether they have been successful, for example, in an attempt to solve a problem.

Current school curricula are often based on error-free learning concepts, in other words, the teacher waits for the one right answer. In life, however, things are usually more complicated. Reflecting this situation, brain researchers stress the importance of developing divergent thinking skills (where all answers are taken into account, and valued, and errors are seen as signs of learning), rather than convergent thinking skills (where there is always just one right answer).

Traditionally speaking, language learning is often less than challenging, cognitively speaking, especially when it comes to beginners' classrooms and very young learners. When a teacher shows a child a picture of a bus and says *Is this a bus?* the answer does not require a lot of thought.

In contrast, tasks aimed at developing thinking skills while developing language skills involve the learners more fully. Language learned through such activities has more meaning for the children, and, as has been proved by both research and experience, will be remembered better. So the activities in this chapter are all aimed at developing not just language, but also basic thinking skills. These skills are important for lifelong learning because they are the building blocks of the more sophisticated thinking capacities that learners need when they are older: logical and critical thinking.

For each activity, you will find the main basic thinking skill involved listed under the *Focus* heading at the beginning. However, note that frequently more than one thinking skill is practised in a single activity. The main basic thinking skills to be developed for this age group have to do with focusing attention, developing memory skills, categorizing, sorting, numeracy, shape recognition, understanding patterns, sequencing, decision-making and imaginative thinking. All these skills are developed in enjoyable ways in the activities that follow.

As a result you can expect to teach a group of happy, interested children, as well as feeling the satisfaction that you are helping them train their brains so they make the most of their lives, wherever the future takes them.

7.1 The *Think!* chant

Outline	Children perform a chant about the importance of focusing and taking time to think.
Focus	Thinking skill: focusing attention
	Language: numbers 1–6, activities (*swimming, running, playing football*), *What is he / she doing? What are they doing? He's / She's / They're (thinking). Wait. Let me think! Just a moment.*
Age	4–6
Time	5–10 minutes
Materials	Pictures of children doing different activities (e.g. swimming, running, playing football, singing), a picture of a child / children thinking.
Preparation	Practise the chant and the actions.

Procedure

1 Show pictures of children doing different activities. Point at one picture and say, e.g. *Look at the children. What are they doing? … They're swimming.* Mime swimming and ask *Can you swim? Show me.* Children do the mime.

2 Repeat with the other pictures. If you don't have pictures, use mime only. Finally, show the picture of a child / children thinking. Ask, e.g. *What's she doing? Is she swimming? No! She isn't swimming. Is she running? Is she playing football?* Mime thinking and say *No. She's thinking.* Explain the meaning of *think* in the children's own language, if necessary.

3 Teach the chant, quietly and rhythmically, with the actions (in brackets).

Wait. Wait.	(make a gesture to mean 'Wait', e.g. holding up one hand)
Let me think!	(mime thinking, e.g. look thoughtful and point to your forehead)
Just a moment.	(point at your watch)
Let me think!	(repeat the mime for thinking)

Note

Helping children to develop their thinking skills is about guiding them to become inquisitive, open-minded and reflective rather than impulsive. This requires the development of a thinking-friendly attitude, and the awareness that they can become better thinkers by making an effort to improve. This activity offers a ritual that initiates a thinking phase and the inner state needed for that. Use the chant whenever you expect your children to be focused on a thinking task, for example, before doing any of the thinking activities in this chapter. It is important that when you do the chant with the children, you give them a good model of being a thinking and reflective person yourself.

7.2 Sorting

Outline	Children sort pasta into bowls according to its shape.
Focus	Thinking skills: comparing, sorting, categorizing
	Language: *pasta, Are they the same or different? They're the same, They're different.*
Age	3–5
Time	5–10 minutes
Materials	Pasta of three to five different shapes (e.g. penne, farfalle, spirali, rotelle and conchiglie), small plastic bowls for each group / table of children (note that you can use other items for sorting – see *Extension ideas*).
Preparation	Put plenty of pasta of different shapes into the bowl for each group to sort. Provide enough bowls to separate out the pasta into the different shapes (i.e. if you have three types, each group needs three empty bowls).

Procedure

1 Demonstrate the activity. Show two pieces of the same kind of pasta and ask *Are they the same or different? … Look. They're the same.* Then show two pieces that are not the same. Say *Look. They're different.* Teach *same* and *different* by holding up more pieces of pasta that are the same shape or a different shape. Encourage the children to join in with the words *same* and *different*.

2 Show children how to put the different pasta shapes into cups according to type.

3 Give a bowl of mixed pasta and enough bowls for the types of pasta to each group. Children work together to sort the pasta. Circulate and encourage them to speak in English as they do so. Ask *Is it the same? Is it different? Look carefully. How many types of pasta have you got?* or say, e.g. *This is the same as bowl one. This is different. This pasta is long.*

4 When they have finished, children show you the separated shapes and then put the pasta back in its original container.

Variations

1 Children sort a mixture of numbers and letters (made of plastic, foam or wood) instead of pasta shapes. They can separate them into number / letter groups or sort them by colour, size, and so on.

2 Prepare cardboard shapes in different colours and sizes (triangles, squares and circles and, for older children, ovals and rectangles). Laminate them if possible. Children sort the shapes into different groups. You can ask *Is it a (triangle)? What shape is it? Is it the same shape?*

Extension ideas

• Once children have done the activity as a class, you could have the pasta shapes on hand in a box for early finishers to sort.

• Pasta shapes can be used for craft activities. Children can paint tube-shaped pasta pieces and then thread them onto string when they are dry, to make necklaces or bracelets. They can also stick pasta shapes to plates or card to make funny faces (with one type of pasta for hair, one type for eyes, another for the mouth, etc.).

7.3 Can you remember?

Outline	Children recall words from vocabulary sets by playing a game with flashcards.
Focus	Thinking skill: developing memory skills
	Language: vocabulary sets (e.g. classroom items, toys, methods of transport, animals), mainly receptive: *Switch on your computer. Focus on the cards. Take one minute. Remember all the cards. What is it? Is it a ...? Yes, it's a ... No, it isn't a ... Let's turn the card(s) over. Let's see who's right. Can you help me, please?*
Age	3–5
Time	10–15 minutes
Materials	Flashcards from various sets of known vocabulary. You will need 9 to 12 flashcards for older children (fewer for three and four year-olds).
	Optional: Tray, cloth, assorted known objects (see *Extension ideas*).
Preparation	None

Procedure

1 The children sit in a circle with you. They help you lay the flashcards face up on the floor inside the circle. Ask *Can you help me, please?* Tell the children to lay out the cards in neat rows and columns, so that each card has its own place.

2 Say *Switch on your computer. Focus on the cards. Take one minute. Remember all the cards.* Time one minute while the children look at the cards and try to remember where each one is.

3 Turn over all of the flashcards so they are face down. Point to one of the cards and ask *What is it?* A child guesses e.g. *It's a car.* Turn the card over. Ask, e.g. *Is it a car?.* If the answer is incorrect (*No, it's a ball.*) turn the card back over. Point to another card and ask *What is it?* When a child guesses the card correctly, say, e.g. *Yes! It's a ball. Well done!* and leave the card face up.

4 Continue in this way with different cards. Leave some time before returning to any cards that have been turned up but guessed incorrectly.

5 Play the game until all the cards are face up.

Extension ideas

- When children are very familiar with the game, use flashcards from two or more vocabulary sets.
- Play 'Can you remember?' using objects on a tray. You need a tray, a cloth to cover it and an assortment of objects which children can name (e.g. a red pen, a blue pen, a yellow crayon, a rubber, three or four different plastic animals, a ball, a toy car). Show the children the tray of objects and ask them to name each one. Put the cloth over the objects and take one away. Remove the cloth, show the tray again and ask *What's missing?* The child who guesses which object has been removed takes the next turn leading the game.

Note

Developing memory is an essential part of children's learning. Holding information in our mind is a pre-requisite for various other thinking skills. In order to remember information well, children need to learn how to focus their attention, and to make associations between individual pieces of information (in this case the position of an item within a network of others).

7.4 What comes next?

Outline	Children revise words with the help of flashcards by putting them into different topic categories.
Focus	Thinking skill: categorizing
	Language: two or more vocabulary sets (e.g. classroom items, toys, transport, animals), *What comes next? That's right. / Well done!*
Age	3–5
Time	10–15 minutes
Materials	Flashcards from various known vocabulary sets.
Preparation	None

Procedure

1   The children sit in a circle with you. Have sets of flashcards ready, organized into topics, such as animals, toys, food and jobs. Hold the flashcards so that the children can see the backs of the cards, not the pictures.

2   Start with the first vocabulary set. Show a flashcard without saying anything and wait for the children to call out the word. When the children have said the word correctly, put the flashcard on the floor face up inside the circle. Take another flashcard from the same set and repeat. Put that card under the first one, to show that it's from the same topic set.

3   Then ask *What comes next?* Wait for the children to call out words. Make sure they know the words should be from the same vocabulary set by saying e.g. *Car? No, Jamie, we're thinking of animals, now, not transport.* When the children have run out of suggestions, show them the next flashcard. Praise any children who guessed the card correctly, e.g. *Well done, Kim!* and put the flashcard on the floor face up with the others of the same vocabulary set.

4   Once all the flashcards from one topic have been put together, show the first card from the next set. Children say the word, e.g. *Bus!* Say *That's right, bus. What comes next?* Once again, hold the flashcard so children can't see the picture, but must go through the transport words they know until someone guesses correctly.

Variation

Play the game with just one flashcard from each vocabulary set. Mime the word on the flashcard for the children to guess. When someone guesses correctly, show the flashcard, then ask *What comes next?* Children call out words from the same vocabulary set until they can't think of any more.

Note

Learning to control information by organizing it into categories helps children to understand the world around them. Categorizing involves various other cognitive skills: comparing and differentiating, focusing attention, and classifying (noticing what makes things belong to the same or different categories).

7.5 Numeracy: *How many dots?*

Outline	Children practise counting and learn to quickly 'see' the numbers on a dice.
Focus	Thinking skill: recognizing numbers
	Language: numbers 1 – 6; *Throw the dice. How many dots (are there)?*
Age	5–7
Time	10–15 minutes
Materials	Two dice (oversized if possible) or digital dice on screen (you can find dice applications on the internet), piece of thick paper or card.
Preparation	None

Procedure

1 The children sit in a circle with you. Put a dice on the floor in the middle of the circle (or show a dice on the whiteboard) so that it shows three dots. Point and count the dots on the dice aloud: *One... two... three.*

2 Now put another dice with five dots showing on the floor next to the first dice (or on the whiteboard). Point at the dice showing five dots. Say *One... two... three... Yes or no?* Give the children only a few seconds, then cover up that dice with a piece of paper so children cannot count the dots. Repeat *One... two... three... Yes or no?* The children call out *Yes* or *No*.

3 Take the paper off the dice. Point and say *Look, we've got one... two... three... four... five.... Five dots on this dice. How many dots are there on that dice? One... two... three... There are three dots on that dice. Five on this dice, and three on that dice.*

4 Continue in this way, putting the two dice in the centre of the circle (or on the whiteboard), one by one, with different numbers of dots showing each time. You will notice that the children gradually join in with your counting, and (if you keep repeating the same phrases) will start using the language themselves. You will also notice, especially if you repeat the game regularly, that children will become more and more confident and precise in recognizing the number of dots on the dice (without actually counting any more).

Variations

1 Ask a child to throw one dice. Give the class a few seconds to grasp the number of dots on the dice, then cover it with a piece of paper or card. Ask *How many dots are there?* Children say what they believe is the number of dots on the dice. Check the number by uncovering the dice.

2 After the children have learned 'same' and 'different' (see 7.2 *Sorting*), get a child to throw two dice instead of one. Again, give the class only a few seconds to grasp the number of dots on each dice, then cover them up. Say *Is the number the same or different?* The children say what they think. Check if the numbers are the same or different by uncovering the dice.

Note

Counting is a basic numerical skill, but children also gradually need to learn to grasp quantities holistically, so they can recognize or estimate numbers without actually counting.

7.6 A six-piece puzzle

Outline	Children make pictures using large and small triangles.
Focus	Thinking skill: shape recognition
	Language: *big, small, triangle, make a(n)... arrow, house, boat, cat, dog, fish*
Age	4–7
Time	10–15 minutes
Materials	Six card triangles for each child (two big and four small), worksheet with pictures to make (see below or the website), an envelope (we recommend a clear plastic one) to store the triangle pieces, sticky tack.
Preparation	Photocopy the puzzle pieces below on card (one set for each child and a set for yourself, if possible larger). Cut each square into six pieces along the lines. Store all the shapes in a clear envelope. Photocopy one worksheet (see page 181 or the website) per child.
	Practise making the different pictures on the worksheet (see page 181) using the six triangles.

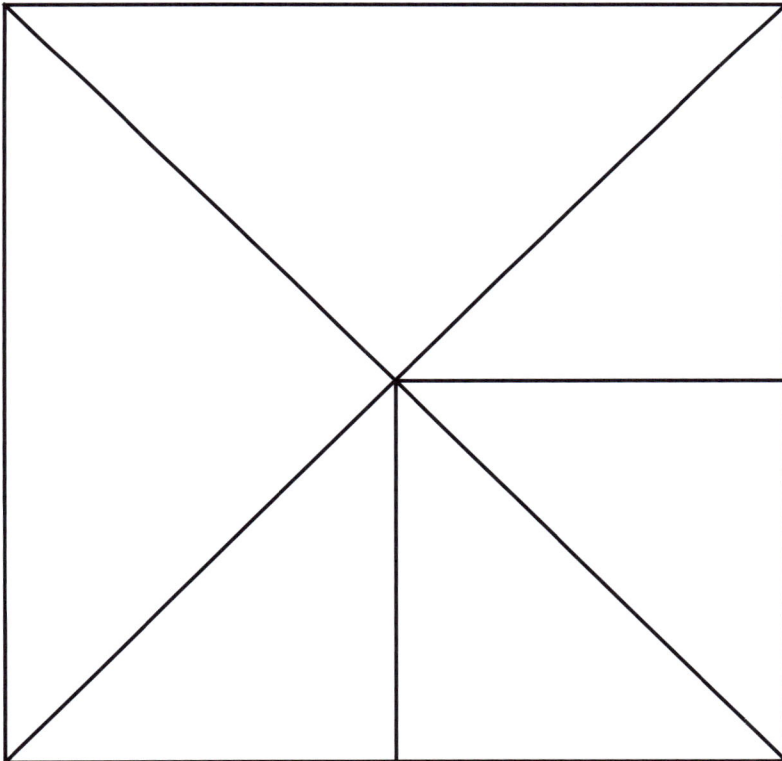

PHOTOCOPIABLE

Procedure

1   Stick your six triangles on the board with sticky tack. Say, e.g. *What are they? … Triangles! How many big triangles? Two! And how many small ones? That's right, four.*

2   Show the worksheet to the children and point at the square. Copy it on the board. Say *Look at the square. I can make the square with my pieces.* Move your triangles on the board to make the square as shown.

3   Hold up the clear envelope and say *Take two big triangles and four small triangles, everyone.* Give out the shapes and check everyone has the correct number of big and small triangles.

4   Go back to your picture on the board. Say *Can you see my square?* Move the pieces around and then say *I'm going to make the square again. Can you do that?* The children try to make the square shape with the triangles on their table. Monitor carefully, helping children who are finding the activity more challenging. Say, e.g. *Look, the big triangles are like this. Can you put the small triangles here? Well done!* It is perfectly acceptable for children to make the shape by arranging their triangles in a different way from you.

5   Give out a worksheet to each child. They work independently to make the pictures with their six triangles. Circulate and give help and praise, e.g. *What are you making, Mariam? The house? Well done! That's great, Sam … A fish!* Tick the box next to each picture on the worksheet as the child completes it. The more often you do this activity, the better children become at recognizing the way they need to put the triangles together to make the pictures.

Variation
Give older children the photocopy of the puzzle pieces to cut up themselves.

Extension ideas
•   Keep the bag of triangle pieces and the worksheets handy. Early finishers can get themselves the pieces they need and work quietly making the pictures by themselves.

•   Once older children have made the pictures a few times, use correction fluid to erase the guidelines showing where the triangles go inside each object on the worksheet. Photocopy the new worksheet and give it to the children with the puzzle pieces. They have to remember / work out how the triangles fit together themselves.

•   Photocopy one picture worksheet for each group. Cut out the pictures and laminate them to make cards. Put them face down in a stack in the middle of each table. Children turn over the cards and make the puzzles. Keep these laminated object cards with the puzzle pieces so that early finishers can refer to them when working independently.

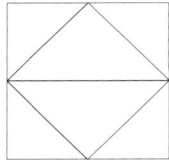

square ☐

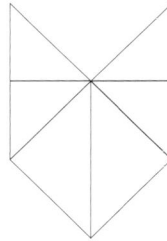

cat ☐

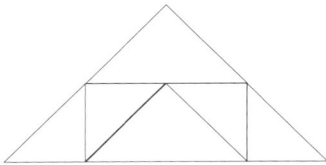

triangle ☐

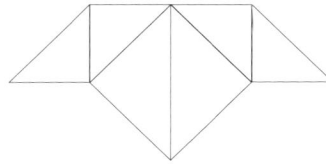

dog ☐

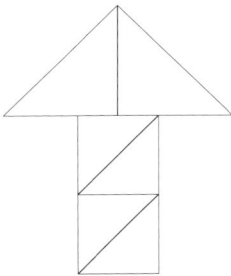

arrow ☐

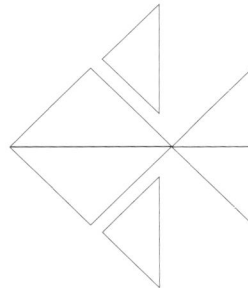

fish ☐

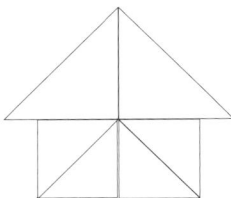

house ☐

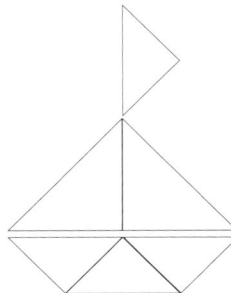

boat ☐

PHOTOCOPIABLE

7.7 Recognizing shapes: puzzles

Outline	Children practise recognizing an image from its parts.
Focus	Thinking skill: problem solving
	Language: revision of known vocabulary (*car, teddy bear, apple*, etc.)
	I think it's …, Maybe it's …, Good idea., I'm not sure.
Age	3–7
Time	10 minutes, over two consecutive lessons
Materials	A4 or A5-sized pictures of objects / animals the children can name in English, envelopes.
Preparation	Cut up the pictures to make puzzles. Put the puzzle pieces for each picture into an envelope.
Note	If you are using printed pictures, it is useful to have two copies of each picture, one to turn into a puzzle, the other one to be used for the word review phase.

Procedure

1 Review the words for the things in the puzzle pictures. Show a completed version of each puzzle picture, if possible, and ask, e.g. *What's this? Is it a (train)?*

2 Hold up one of the envelopes with puzzles inside. Show children one puzzle piece from the envelope, for example, a piece of a car picture. Put it on the table or stick it on the board, so all the children can see it well. Don't say anything: just wait for the children to suggest a word for the whole picture. If a child says *car*, ask the rest of the class *What do you think? Good idea? Yes or no?*

3 Take out another puzzle piece from the same envelope and put it on the table / board. Say *What do you think? Maybe it's a plane. A plane? Yes or no?* Children are likely to say *No* or *No plane. Car.* React by showing interest, but do not immediately say whether the children are right or wrong.

4 Take out another piece from the same envelope. Say *I think it's a cat!* If you say this in a joking way, children will often react by laughing and protesting loudly *No, no. No cat. Car.* Again, you can use their responses to scaffold their language. Say, for example, *Oh, I see. You think it's a car. It isn't a cat, is it? No. It really isn't a cat!*

5 Gradually, put the puzzle together on the table / board with the children's help. Encourage them by asking, e.g. *Where do I put this? Here? Next to that one?*

6 Repeat this procedure for the other puzzles.

Variation

Divide the class into groups. Put a puzzle (with the pieces mixed up) on each table. Children complete the puzzle in their group. Monitor, asking *What's this? What do you think? Where do you put this?* and encouraging the children to speak English. When a group has finished, you check the puzzle. Then they take it apart and mix up the pieces. The children change tables in their groups when you tell them to, moving on to another puzzle.

Note

Putting a puzzle together promotes hand-eye coordination and fine motor skills. Figuring out whether a piece fits or doesn't fit helps to develop important spatial and visual strategies (such as noticing, pattern recognition, and identification of details). Children learn to engage in a step-by-step approach to solving problems.

7.8 Recognizing shapes: counting

Outline	Children count shapes or objects that overlap in a picture.
Focus	Thinking skill: shape recognition
	Language: numbers 1–6, shapes, *What can you see in the picture? Are there three or five (triangles)? How many (circles) can you see?*
Age	5–7
Time	10–15 minutes
Materials	Flashcards to revise the words you wish to practise (shapes or other objects), a copy of Worksheet A for each child (see page 184 or the website).
	Variation: Worksheet B (see page 185 or the website).
Preparation	Photocopy one or both of the worksheets.

Procedure

1 Use flashcards and multi-sensory activities to revise shapes (*circle, triangle, square*).

2 Revise numbers one to six. Hold a number of pencils (between one and six) behind your back. Say *How many pencils are there?* Wait for the children to make their guesses. Then say *OK, let's see.* Count the number of pencils with the class. Repeat with different numbers of pencils, until you notice that the children have no problem saying the numbers.

3 Hand out Worksheet A. Tell the children they have to find out how many circles, squares and triangles there are. Put the children in pairs and encourage them to count the shapes together (in English).

4 When pairs have finished counting, get the attention of the class. Then ask questions about the picture, e.g. *Are there three or five triangles? How many squares can you see?*

Variation

Copy Worksheet B. Get the children to count items from a lexical set instead of shapes. This time the items are only partially seen, rather than overlapping. Ask, e.g. *What can you see? Where can you see a bus? Ah, that's good. How many buses are there? Are there two, three or five planes?*

Note

This activity requires a combination of basic numerical skills and the ability to identify shapes and to focus attention. As the children count the overlapping shapes or parts of pictures, they will also need to use their short-term memory in order to come up with meaningful answers.

> ♀ **Tip**
>
> See Puchta / Williams, *Teaching Young Learners to Think* (Helbling Photocopiable Resources, 2011), pages 80–81, for more challenging ideas to get children to find hidden shapes in a picture.

A

PHOTOCOPIABLE

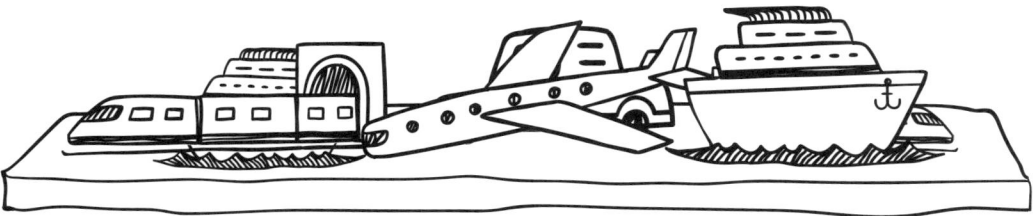

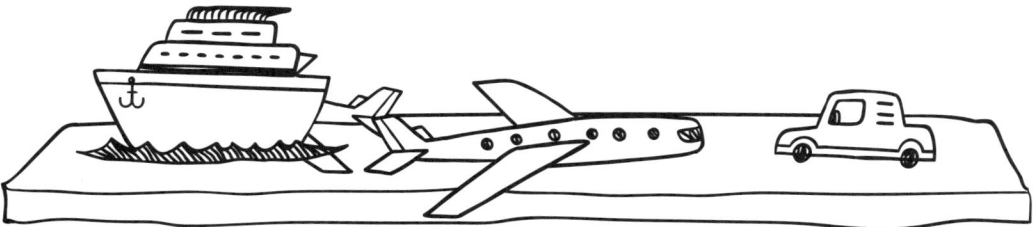

B

PHOTOCOPIABLE

7.9 Understanding patterns

Outline	Children practise identifying patterns in a series of pictures.
Focus	Thinking skill: understanding patterns Language: revision of vocabulary sets (e.g. animals, classroom items, weather)
Age	6–7
Time	15 minutes
Materials	Printed clip art pictures or pictures from the internet and a piece of paper with a large question mark drawn on it. You will need several copies of each picture.
Preparation	Work out some patterns with the pictures you have before the class (see examples below).

Procedure

1 Put pictures from the same vocabulary set on the floor, or stick them on the board. Arrange the pictures in a simple repeating pattern (not too easy for your class and not too challenging). Instead of the last picture in the pattern, put a question mark, for example:

Figure 7.1: Pictures arranged in a repeating pattern

2 Point at the pictures, and say the words rhythmically to help the children detect a pattern:

Mouse, mouse, rabbit (stress the word *rabbit*)
Mouse, mouse, ...

Pause and wait for the children to say the next word in the pattern (*rabbit*).

3 The children stand in a circle with you. Say the pattern again, rhythmically as before:

Mouse, mouse, rabbit,
Mouse, mouse, rabbit.

4 Gesture as if you are handing the pattern of words to the child on your right. Encourage the child to say the pattern, and then pass it on to the child to their right, in the same way. Repeat until all the children have said the pattern.

Variations

Here are more examples of patterns you can use:

Figure 7.2: More examples of repeating patterns

Note

Recognizing patterns is an important cognitive skill needed in, for example, problem solving and scientific thinking. In this activity, children learn to understand and complete sequences of pictures. In order to do that successfully, they need to identify a certain pattern, work out the changes that occur from one item to the next in a sequence, and draw conclusions from the pattern to decide what comes next.

7.10 What's the right order?

Outline	Children look at a series of pictures from a story and put them in the correct order.
Focus	Thinking skill: sequencing
	Language: *What's the order? Is this the order? Is this OK? Is this better?* numbers 1–3, language describing a sequence of actions (receptive only)
Age	5–7
Time	10–15 minutes over three consecutive lessons
Materials	Photocopy the pictures for one of the stories on the following pages (or on the website).
Preparation	Stick the pictures onto card and cut each story into separate pictures. Practise talking about the pictures.

Procedure

1   Put the three pictures for one of the stories (e.g. Story 1) on the table or on the board in random order. Give the children time to look at the pictures. Encourage them to say what they can see, prompting when necessary, e.g. *What can you see in this picture? … That's right. It's a cat. Where is it? Is it in a house?* When the children comment on the pictures using their own language, scaffold their language by repeating what they have said in English and commenting on it (see *Go beyond an input–output model of learning*, Introduction page 9).

2   When the children run out of things to say, ask *What's the order?* Put the pictures in a sequence that is clearly not possible. Say *Is this OK? Yes or no? Number one… two… three.* Move the pictures around and ask *Or is this better? One… two…three. What do you think? What's the order?*

3   Encourage one of the children to come to the front and put the pictures in the order they think works best. See if the rest of the class agree, and repeat until everyone agrees on the order. Then go through the story, commenting on the pictures, using mime, gestures and the images to aid the children's comprehension. See below for suggested stories to go with the three sets of pictures on pages 189–191 (actions in brackets).

4   Repeat the process with the other two stories in the next two lessons.

Extension idea

Use the same strategies to work on stories about pictures you have drawn or found yourself.

Note

Being able to carry things out in sequential order is important in many areas of life. We need to make sure that soup is the right temperature before we can eat it. We need to take an umbrella before we leave the house when it looks like rain, and so on. Children need to learn to keep to sequences, too, in many areas of language: when they tell a story, when they give instructions or when they explain something, for example. In any of these areas, a lack of sequential thinking would lead to confusion.

Story 1

Look at picture number one. There is a cat in the tree (make a cat noise) *and the cat's scared. She's so scared.* (act scared) *Poor cat! But look. The man has got a mobile phone.* (mime holding a mobile phone) *He can see the cat.* (point at your eyes and the cat in the picture) *He takes his mobile phone and he talks to the fire brigade.* (mime making a phone call) *He says 'Hello, hello, we've got a problem. There's a cat in the tree. She's so scared.'*

Look here. This is picture number two. There's the fire brigade. (make the noise of a fire engine's siren) *The fire brigade comes to help the cat. The cat's still in the tree. And the cat's scared. She's so scared.* (act scared)

Now picture number three. The fire brigade have got a big ladder, and they put it up against the tree. (mime moving a heavy ladder) *This firefighter climbs up the ladder,* (mime climbing a ladder) *and she helps the cat. Is the cat still scared? No, not any more. The cat's happy.* (act happy) *She's so happy.*

From *Activities for Very Young Learners* © Cambridge University Press 2017   PHOTOCOPIABLE

Story 2

Look. It's morning. Ah, there are dark clouds. Look at the clouds. (point at them in picture one and draw dark clouds on the board) *This is Timmy. He's going out. And here's his mum. She's got an umbrella for Timmy.* (mime holding and opening an umbrella) *She says, 'This umbrella is for you, Timmy. Look at the clouds!'*

And now look at this picture here. What about the clouds? There are no clouds any more. Look. It's sunny. (draw a sun on the board) *Ah! It's sunny and warm. And here's Timmy. He's happy.* (act happy) *But where's the umbrella? Look, it's here.* (point to the umbrella)

Look at picture three. Is it sunny? No, it isn't. It's raining. (mime being out in the rain / draw rain on the board) *Look at Timmy. Poor Timmy! There's rain on his head. There's rain on his face. There's rain on his nose.* (point to the different parts of the body as you mention them and mime being wet through) *There's a lot of rain!*

From *Activities for Very Young Learners* © Cambridge University Press 2017   PHOTOCOPIABLE

Story 3

Look at this girl. Her name's Emily. Is she happy? Yes! She's eating. (mime eating) *What's she eating? She's eating a peach.* (mime picking a peach from a tree and draw a peach on the board) *It's good. Yummy!*

And now look. Emily's got a flower pot. She puts the peach stone in the pot. Look. Here's the peach stone. Emily puts it in the pot. (mime planting a peach stone)

Look at picture three. There's a little plant. Wow! Emily is giving it some water. (mime watering a plant) *How nice! Look. She's very happy.*

7.11 Would you rather?

Outline	Children practise making choices quickly.
Focus	Thinking skill: decision-making
	Language: *This, please. Thank you.* Receptive: *What would you rather have? The (teddy bear) or the (doll)? Here you are. That's OK. / You're welcome.*
Age	6–7
Time	15–20 minutes
Materials	Board or flip chart, chalk or felt tips, pairs of flashcards for children to choose between, e.g. a teddy bear / a doll; the sun / the moon; a dog / a cat.
	Optional: Pictures or flashcards of different places (e.g. a beach, mountains, a tree hut, a tent, a hotel, an igloo); different foods, different clothes or different modes of transport (see *Variations*).
Preparation	None

Procedure

1   Offer a confident child two different flashcards, e.g. a teddy bear and a doll, and ask *What would you rather have? The teddy bear or the doll?*

2   Let the child choose. Encourage them to say, e.g. *This, please.* or *The doll, please.* Then hand over the flashcard. Say *Here you are.* Encourage the child to say *Thank you* and respond with *That's OK. / You're welcome.*

3   Continue in this way with all the children. If a child is not able to say the word for the item yet, it is perfectly acceptable for them to say just *This*, or simply point at their choice. In that case, scaffold the child's language by saying, e.g. *Ah, you want the teddy bear. The teddy bear. OK.*

4   Once the children are familiar with the phrase *Would you rather…?* you can challenge them by asking which of three options they would rather have.

Variations

1   Offer children stickers rather than flashcards so they can keep the item they choose.

2   Vary the choices and language by using different vocabulary sets. Show pictures or flashcards of places and ask children *Where would you rather be?* Show pictures of types of food and ask *What would you rather eat?* Show pictures of different items of clothing and ask *What would you rather wear?* or show methods of transport and ask *How would you rather travel?*

Note

Making the right decision when faced with a choice is not always easy for children. They may want both options, or they may be unable to decide. This activity gives them practice in decision-making in a fun and non-threatening way. Small children love this activity and they may surprise you by choosing the option which seems less appealing to an adult!

7.12 The magic box

Outline	Children listen to instructions with their eyes closed and practise visualizing.
Focus	Thinking skill: imaginative thinking
	Language: revision of vocabulary, colours, numbers
	Receptive: *This is my magic box. What's in it? I can see … In my magic box there is / are … That's your magic box. What's in your magic box?*
Age	4–6
Time	10–15 minutes
Materials	Soft, relaxing music, a sheet of paper and crayons for each child.
Preparation	Make a 'magic box' by covering a cardboard box with colourful paper and decorating it with stickers, glitter, etc.

Procedure

1   Show the children your magic box. Ask them if they want to find out what's inside. Say, e.g. *Look at this box. Do you like it? It's very special. Very, very special. It's a magic box. A magic box. Do you want to know what's in it? OK, close your eyes and listen. Listen carefully.* You could use the sandwiching technique to help children to understand better what you are saying, e.g. say a sentence in English, then in the children's own language, and then in English again.

2   Tell the children to find a comfortable position. This could be lying on the floor on their backs, if that is possible in your classroom (say *Lie down everyone. Close your eyes.*) or resting their heads on their arms on the desk in front of them (say *Cross your arms. Put your head on your arms. Close your eyes.*)

3   Play some gentle music at a low volume. Describe what's in your magic box, using a soft voice, almost whispering, but making sure all the children in the class can hear you. Use vocabulary the children have learned recently, and only structures that the children are very familiar with. Say, for example:

> *This is my magic box.*
> *What's in it?*
> *One… two… three…*
> *Oh! I can see a blue train.*
> *In my magic box … there is a blue train.*

> or
> *Here's my magic box.*
> *What's in it?*
> *Abracadabra!*
> *Wizzy wizzy woo!*
> *My box is now open,*
> *It's open for you.*
> *Oh! Wow!*
> *There are three big lollies.*
> *They are green, yellow, blue and red.*
> *Yummy!*

4   Give each child a piece of paper and crayons. Play the same gentle music again. Ask the children to close their eyes and imagine they've got a magic box. Say:

> *You've got a magic box.*
> *Ah! It's beautiful.*
> *What's in it?*
> *What's in your magic box?*

5   Give children time to enjoy this quiet phase. Gently ask them to open their eyes. Say *What's in your magic box? Pick up your crayons. Draw!* Explain in the children's own language that they need to draw what they imagined in the box.

6   The children show their finished drawings to you and to each other. Depending on the language level of the class, you can either comment on the drawings or get the children to tell you what their pictures show.

Extension ideas

• Put all the drawings in a magic box to open and show to children during circle time over the next couple of classes. Comment on the drawings by saying what you like about them, talking about the colours or other details.

• Display the drawings on a magic box poster for everyone to see.

• Play a mystery box guessing game. Put something in a box and ask children to guess what it is. Give them clues, e.g. *It's small, you use it with a pencil, you use it like this* (mime rubbing something out). Children guess, e.g. *It's a rubber.*

Note

This activity helps children to develop their imaginative thinking and the ability to conceive images, which according to neuro-biologists is at the core of the creative process.

8   Pronunciation and early literacy

Teachers and parents often comment on young children's ability to repeat songs, chants and rhymes almost perfectly. Current research also confirms that young children find it easier than older learners to pick up the sounds of a foreign language. This means that the early learner classroom provides a great opportunity to expose children to the many sounds of English.

In this chapter we start with activities to develop phonological awareness, encouraging young learners to hear the qualities of different sounds and to practise the phonemes of the English language. These are followed by activities which practise stress and intonation patterns (of course, songs, chants and many games also provide this kind of practice).

Pronunciation and literacy are closely related, since phonological awareness is a major factor in learning to read and write in an alphabetic language such as English. The early reading activities provided here are based on a phonics approach. The letters in the English alphabet can be pronounced in a number of ways and a common complaint from older learners is that they can't tell how to pronounce a word from the way it's written. However, we can help young learners to become familiar with the most common pronunciations of English letters, since recognizing letter-sound relationships is an important step in learning to read and write.

It is important that children get used to saying the most common phonemes for the letters of the alphabet, rather than their letter names. This is to enable them to sound out the letters and blend sounds in order to read some words straight away. It is also worth noting that learning these relationships helps children to remember and pronounce phonemes and combinations of phonemes which don't occur in their own language. Phonics also helps children develop their 'edging' skill – the ability to hear where one word ends and another begins.

Although it is outside of the scope of this book to provide a comprehensive phonics programme, the activities provided in this chapter can be used on their own or as supplementary material to help very young children develop their early reading skills.

The last three activities will help you create English 'literacy events' as part of your lessons. Ticking items off a shopping list, making books and writing letters together as a class give very young children the opportunity to begin to participate in the written world in a fun and meaningful way.

8.1 The body percussion game

Outline	Children make softer and louder noises in order to practise distinguishing between sounds.
Focus	*Can you ...? clap, slap, stamp (your feet), tap (your foot), louder, softer*
Age	3–7
Time	5–10 minutes
Materials	None
Preparation	None

Procedure

1 Stand in a circle with the children. Say *Can you clap?* Demonstrate clapping and say *Clap, clap, clap.* The children copy.
2 Say *Louder!* and clap more loudly. The children copy. Say *Softer!* and clap more quietly. The children copy.
3 Say *Can you slap your legs?* Demonstrate and say *Slap, slap, slap.* The children copy. Slap more loudly and more quietly, saying *Louder! Softer!* as before. The children copy.
4 Do the same with *Can you stamp your feet?* and *Can you tap your foot?*
5 Then put all the actions together. Say *Clap, slap, stamp, tap, tap, tap! Clap, slap, stamp, tap, tap, tap!* The children do the actions with you several times. Ask them to change the volume by saying *Louder!* or *Softer!*
6 Finish the activity by whispering the instructions and doing the four actions very slowly and quietly. The children copy you and may begin to say the words, too.

Variations

1 Change *Louder! Softer!* to *Faster! Slower!*
2 With older children add *Can you click your fingers?* or *Can you click your tongue?* Varying the instructions and asking the children to do things louder, softer, slower or faster brings a lot of fun (and some chaos!) to the activity.

8.2 Animal noises

Outline	Children practise English phonemes through animal sounds, experimenting with pitch, loudness and length.
Focus	*cat, dog, cow, mouse, miaow, woof, moo, squeak, What animal is this / it? A (cat) says …*
Age	3–5
Time	5–10 minutes
Materials	Flashcards of animals that make noises (e.g. cat, dog, cow and mouse), a large envelope.
Preparation	None

Procedure

1   Show an animal flashcard, for example, a cat, and ask *What animal is this? … Yes, it's a cat.* or say *Look! A cat!* Say, e.g. *A cat says …* and make the English animal noise *Miaow!* The children repeat the noise.

2   Do the same with the other animal flashcards. Note that we often repeat the noises made by dogs and mice at least twice (*Woof! Woof! Squeak! Squeak!*) but *Miaow!* and *Moo!* have very long vowel sounds, so we tend to say them just once at a time.

3   Practise all the animal noises several times.

4   Hold one of the flashcards so the children can't see it and make the English animal noise. Ask *What animal is it?* Children guess.

5   Children take turns to come to the front and make an English animal sound for the rest of the class to guess. With large classes, choose three or four children at a time to come up and make the animal noise together. They will think this is great fun.

6   Once children know the animal sounds, play a game. Put all the flashcards in an envelope. Children make a circle. Pull a flashcard out of the envelope, and without showing the card to the children say, e.g. *Be a dog.* The children make the appropriate noise (e.g. *Woof! Woof!*) and can also mime being the animal. Show the flashcard to confirm that they are making the right noise. Then pull another flashcard out of the envelope.

Variation

Include other animals, for example, pig (*Oink!*), snake (*Hiss!*), frog (*Croak!*), sheep (*Baa!*), chick (*Cheep! Cheep!*), hen (*Cluck! Cluck!*) and duck (*Quack! Quack!*).

Extension ideas

* If you need to form groups, point and say an animal for each child, e.g. (for 12 children) *cat, dog, cow, mouse, cat, dog, cow, mouse, cat, dog, cow, mouse.* Children form groups of the same animal, and after making the animal noise together, they sit in their new group.

* Sing *Old MacDonald had a farm.* Besides the animal sounds, children practise some long vowels when they sing *E, I, E, I, O!*

* Sing a finger puppet song. You will need five animal finger puppets, one for each finger. Make a fist, with the puppet heads facing into your palm (or hide your hand behind a chair). As you sing the song, hold up or show each finger puppet, e.g. *Where is cat? Where is cat? Here I am! Here I am! Miaow, Miaow, Miaow!* Then hide the puppet again and sing, e.g. *Goodbye cat! Goodbye cat!*

Continue with the next finger puppet, for example, *Where is dog? Where is dog? Here I am! Here I am! Woof, woof, woof! Goodbye dog! Goodbye dog!* and so on.

Note
Children find it fascinating that animal sounds in English are often different from those in their own language. This is because the animal sounds children learn reflect the phonological patterns of their first language, and are in fact usually part of a baby's introduction to his or her own language. Within these animal noise words there are likely to be phonemes which do not exist in the children's first language.

8.3 The first sounds team game

Outline	Children practise identifying the initial sounds in words by playing a team game.
Focus	Ten words that begin with the sounds /b/, /k/, /f/, /h/ and /s/ (e.g. *book, banana, cake, cat, fish, flower, hat, house, sandwich, sun*), *I see something beginning with …*
Age	4–7
Time	10 minutes to play the game. You will need to present the first sounds in the words over a few lessons before you play the game.
Materials	Two flashcards each of words that begin with the sounds /b/, /k/, /f/, /h/ and /s/. Optional: Two plastic flyswatters.
Preparation	Photocopy the cards on page 201 if you do not have ten flashcards. Find more pictures and / or objects in the classroom which start with the sounds /b/, /k/, /f/, /h/ and /s/ (e.g. ball, bag, cupboard, cup, frog, the number four, head, hand, snake, sock).

Procedure

1 Present the phonemes in different lessons, one at a time. Start with the sound /b/. Hold up the book flashcard and ask *What's this?* … Say *That's right, it's a book. Listen b b b book!* Children listen and repeat.

2 Hold up the banana flashcard. Say *b b b banana*. Children listen and repeat. Mime looking for another object which starts with the same sound. Point to a bag and say, e.g. *b b b bag!* Children repeat. Elicit other words which start with /b/, such as *ball, boy*.

3 Present the other four sounds in the same way, over consecutive lessons.

4 When the children are familiar with the five phonemes (/b/, /k/, /f/, /h/ and /s/), play a version of activity 2.13 *Flyswatter fun* (see page 67). Put the ten flashcards on the board in random order. Divide the class into two teams.

5 The teams line up facing the flashcards. If using, give the first child in each team a flyswatter. If playing without flyswatters; children slap the cards with their hands (but the flashcards fall off the board much more easily without flyswatters).

6 Say *I see something beginning with /s/*. The two children at the front of the teams run and try to slap a flashcard on the wall which starts with the sound /s/ with the flyswatter (or their hand).

7 Each child can only slap one flashcard, so they both have the opportunity to find a flashcard starting with the sound (e.g. if you say /s/, one child will touch the picture of the sun and the other the sandwich). Children in the line can help by saying the objects starting with the sound.

8 The children at the front of the teams go to the back and the two children who are now at the front play the next round (with a different sound). Repeat until everyone has had a go, then play the game all over again – but faster!

Extension ideas

- Create an *Our first sounds* wall display. When you or the children find a new word that starts with one of the sounds you have practised, add a picture of it to the display.

- Play a version of activity 2.10 *What's in the bag?* (see page 64) with sounds. Put an object that starts with each of the sounds /b/, /k/, /f/, /h/ and /s/ in a bag (e.g. a ball, a toy cat, a plastic flower, a toy horse and a toy snake). Put your hand in the bag and take hold of one of the objects. Say the sound (without showing the object). The children guess the object by saying things that start with the sound. When they guess correctly, pull the object out of the bag to show them. When they are familiar with the game, children can take turns choosing an object from the bag. Younger children say the name of the object (while the class says the sound), older ones say the initial sound for the rest of the class to guess the object.

- Play the *Sounds Shops* game with older children. Show them a picture of a shop and draw a simple shop on the board. Say, e.g. *My name's Pete. I sell pencils.* Draw a pencil near the shop. Elicit what else you could sell in your shop (everything must start with the same sound as your name (*Pete*)), e.g. *pens, paper, pears.* The children draw their own shop. They think about a sound they know, choose a name for themselves beginning with the sound and think about things they could sell (starting with the same sound). They draw the items in or around their picture. They take turns to tell the class about their shops, e.g. *I'm Mike. I sell monkeys. I sell monsters. I sell mice. I sell mangos. Come to my shop. It's fantastic!* You may have to give the children English names if the sounds are not the same in their language.

💡 **Tip**

When teaching initial sounds to three year-olds, start with one consonant sound only. Once they can say (or point to) items starting with that sound, add another. When you have covered each consonant sound separately, review two of them in one lesson, and so on, so that by the end of the year, children have learned to hear and say words starting with different consonant sounds.

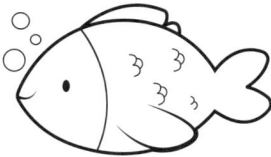 

 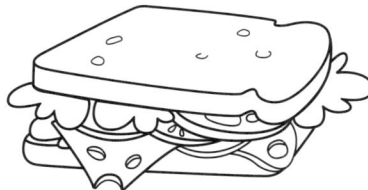

PHOTOCOPIABLE

8.4 New phonemes: a rhyming finger play

Outline	Children practise phonemes not found in their own language using a well-known rhyme.
Focus	The sound /h/, *Hickory dickory dock, mouse, mice, run up, clock, run down*
Age	3–7
Time	5 minutes
Materials	None
Preparation	Practise saying the rhyme and doing the actions.

Procedure

1 Hold your left hand up, bent at the elbow so that your palm is flat and facing the children. Say *Can you see the clock?* Point to a real clock. Then make a circle in the middle of your palm with your right hand to show that your hand is representing a clock. Say *This is the clock*.

2 Hold up the three middle fingers on your right hand. Say *These are the mice*. Point to and move each finger in turn and say *Mouse one. Squeak! Squeak! Mouse two. Squeak! Squeak! Mouse three. Squeak! Squeak!*

3 Say *This is the story 'Hickory, dickory, dock'!* Break the name down so children can practise it. Say *H – h – h – hickory*. The children repeat. *Dickory* (children repeat) *dock* (children repeat). Say the whole phrase *Hickory, dickory, dock!* (children repeat).

4 Teach the rhyme line by line, with the actions (shown in brackets). The children first copy the actions, then join in with the words.

Hickory, dickory, dock,	(wriggle your three 'mouse' fingers)
The mice run up the clock,	(run your three fingers up your forearm to the 'clock face' – your palm)
The clock strikes one – bong!	(with the mice still at the clock face, drop your fingers onto the palm of your hand as you say *Bong!*)
And down they run,	(move your fingers down the other side of your forearm as if the mice are running away)
Hickory, dickory, dock!	(move your hands back to the starting position)

5 Repeat the rhyme over a few classes. If you hear children mispronouncing /h/, practise the sound on its own and at the beginning of the word *Hickory*.

Variations

1 Practise the sound /r/ with the following rhyme:

Rain, rain! Go away!	(wiggle your fingers to show rain and make a gesture for 'Go away!')
Come again another day!	(make a 'Come here!' gesture)
Can you see we want to play?	(make a questioning gesture and jump up and down)
Rain, rain! Go away!	(repeat the actions for the first line)

2   Practise the sound /p/ with the following rhyme:

Two little birds sitting on a wall,	(hold your two index fingers up with the rest of the fingers folded out of view)
One named Peter, one named Paul.	(hold up each index finger in turn as if one is called Peter and the other Paul)
Fly away Peter! Fly away Paul!	(move the 'Peter' index finger behind your back as if it is a bird flying away, then do the same with the other index finger)
Come back Peter! Come back Paul!	(bring the 'Peter' index finger back to the starting position, then the other index finger)

Note

You can use many traditional rhymes and songs to practise sounds that your children don't have in their own language. Invent a sequence of actions to go with the rhyme or song you choose, paying special attention to the target sound or sounds.

8.5 The *Whisper it!* game

Outline	Children practise simple sentence stress by playing a whispering game. This game is suitable for small classes only.
Focus	Four countable nouns from a known vocabulary set, e.g. toys: *ball, doll, kite, robot*, lists with *and* (e.g. *A bike, a robot and a doll.*)
Age	4–7
Time	10–15 minutes
Materials	Four flashcards from a vocabulary set (e.g. toys, animals, transport, classroom items).
Preparation	None

Procedure

1 Sit in a circle with the children. Show one of the four flashcards and ask *What's this?* Children reply, e.g. *A ball.* Encourage them to repeat the phrase, e.g. *A ball.* Do the same with the other three flashcards.

2 Put all the flashcards face down in a pile. Say *Listen.* Take two flashcards, look at them and hold them so that the children can't see the pictures. Whisper a phrase with the two words on the cards to the child on your right, e.g. *A bike and a robot.* Indicate that the child must whisper the phrase to the child sitting on their right. The next child whispers the phrase to the child sitting on their right, and so on, around the circle.

3 Ask the last child in the circle before you *What have I got?* They say the phrase out loud (*A bike and a robot*). Hold up the flashcards and say, e.g. *A bike and a robot!*

4 Pick up another flashcard from the pile. Repeat the game, but this time add the extra word to the phrase you whisper to the child on your right, e.g. *A bike, a robot and a doll.*

5 Play the game again, this time with all four flashcards (the children say, e.g. *A kite, a robot, a doll and a ball.*). Keep playing, changing the order and number of objects you say.

Variations

1 Very young children love playing this game with one word. Once they understand the game, use two or three words at a time.

2 With older children who know prepositions (*in, on, under*), use picture cards showing objects in different positions, for example, a cat in a bag. Whisper the phrase in the same way (e.g. *A cat in a bag*). Then ask the last child in the circle *What is it?* They say the phrase. Show the picture to check. Children say, e.g. *It's a cat in a bag!*

8.6 Learning letter-sound relationships

Outline	Children become familiar with the most common letter-sound correspondences for the letters of the English alphabet.
Focus	Simple words beginning with the first sound children learn for each letter of the alphabet, e.g. *a – ant, b – bag, c – cat, d – dog, e – egg*
Age	4–7
Time	5 minutes in each class (presenting one letter-sound correspondence)
Materials	Letter-sound cards and picture flashcards.
Preparation	Photocopy the set of cards on pages 206–207 or see the website. Practise saying the letter sounds before you present them. Some are pronounced in a long and continuous manner, e.g. *f* /fffff/, *m* /mmmm/ and *s* /ssss/. We need to add a slight schwa to say the voiced phonemes in isolation, e.g. b /bə/, d /də/ and r /rə/. Examples of unvoiced short phonemes are c /k/, k /k/ and h /h/. The short vowel sounds a, e, i, o and u are monophthongs.

Procedure

1 Hold up the *b* flashcard (not the picture) and say the sound /b/. Show the book picture flashcard and ask *What's this?* Say *Yes, it's a book. Listen: b b book.* Children repeat the sound and the word. Ask children to tell you other words that start with the same sound (e.g. *ball, boy, board, bike, bear, bathroom, banana*).

2 Present the rest of the 26 alphabet letter-sound correspondences in consecutive lessons. You could have a regular 'Let's read' slot at the beginning of every lesson or during circle time.

3 Once you have taught the letter sounds, use part of circle time in each class for initial sounds work. Hold up a letter flashcard, e.g. *s* and say *What's the sound? Ssss! I can see something starting with ssss.* Look around the room and point to something beginning with the sound which children can say in English (e.g. a picture of a star). Say *That's right. It's a star.* Encourage the children to spot more things beginning with the sound, e.g. *Yes, Inma! The sun starts with ssss. What can you see Jon? A snake! Very good.*

4 Play matching games with the letter and picture flashcards until the children can automatically remember the letter sounds (see *Extension ideas*, below).

Extension ideas

• Photocopy and cut up a set of the letter cards (without the pictures or words). Stick the picture and word flashcards on the walls. Give out the letter cards to the children one by one. They take turns to say the letter sound on their card and match it to one of the picture flashcards on the wall.

• Play *Phonics I spy / I can see…* . The game is similar to regular *I spy*, but you say the phoneme at the beginning of the word you are thinking of, not the name of the letter. Remember that the letters *c* and *k* represent the same sound (/k/) and are interchangeable. They are alternative spellings for the same sound. If you say *I can see something starting with /k/ /k/ /k/*, both *cat* and *kite* will be correct answers. If you want to distinguish between the two letters, hold up the *c* letter flashcard while you say the sound (then only words starting with the letter *c* will be correct).

• Make a wall display to help children read and remember the letter-sound correspondences and words that start with the sounds. Put the letter-sound flashcards on the wall. Add pictures of new words under each letter-sound as the children learn them.

a	b	c	d
e	f	g	h
i	j	k	l
m	n	o	p
q	r	s	t
u	v	w	x
y	z		

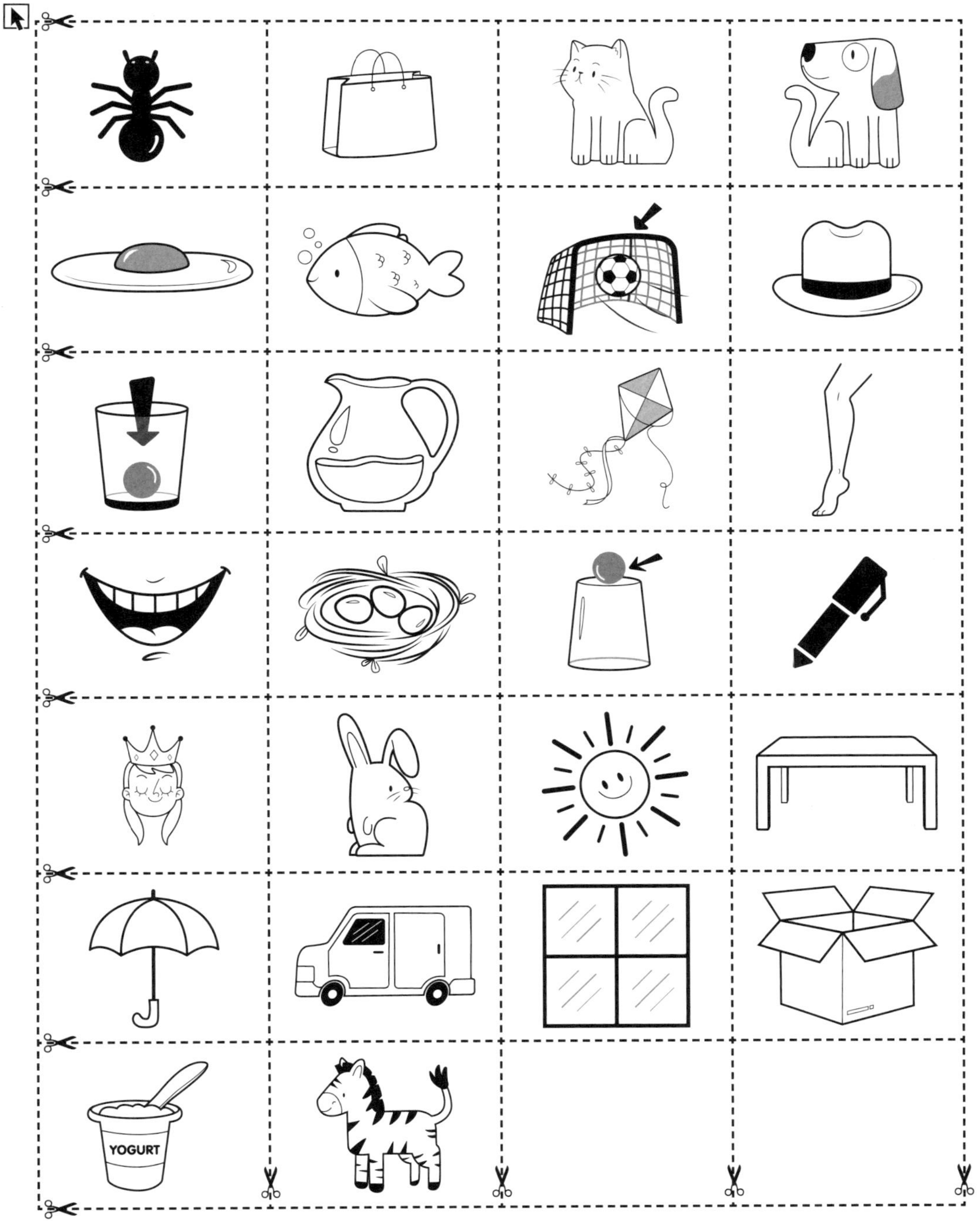
YOGURT

8.7 Blending and word endings: *at, en, ox*

Outline	Children learn to blend letter sounds and identify the ending sounds in some words.
Focus	Using the word cards *cat*, *hat*, *pen*, *ten*, *box* and *fox* children listen, read and say beginning, middle and ending sounds in these words. They read the x letter sound /ks/ at the end of words (this letter sound is never found at the beginning of a word e.g. *six, taxi, exit*).
Age	5–7
Time	10–20 minutes
Materials	One set of picture cards for you, (enlarged if possible), a copy of the cards on page 209 for each child or pair of children, an envelope, sticky tack, scissors.
Preparation	Prepare a set of the picture cards on page 209 (or see the website) for yourself and put them in an envelope. Make copies of page 209 (with the three sets of cards) or see the website.

Procedure

1 Give each child or pair of children a worksheet and scissors. Children cut along the dotted lines to make the three sets of cards (word endings, letters and pictures).

2 Once the cards are cut up, ask children to put them in three piles.

3 Start by revising the letter sounds. Children put the letter cards in a row in front of them. They point to and repeat each letter sound after you (/b/, /k/, /f/, /h/, /p/, /t/).

4 Next ask the children to lay out the word ending cards. Say *a – t, at, e – n, en* and *o – x, ox*. Children point to the cards and repeat after you. They keep the letter cards and word ending cards in front of them.

5 Pull a picture card out of your envelope. Don't let children see the card. Say, e.g. *It's a cat ... c – a – t.* Write *cat* on the board. *Put 'c' in front of 'at'.* Children put the correct cards together. Say *Very good!* Show them the picture of the cat.

6 Pull the next picture out of the envelope. Say, e.g. *Now, what's this? It's a pen! p-e-n. Can you make pen? Great.* Write *pen* on the board under *cat.* Say *Put it under cat.*

7 Continue until you've pulled all the pictures out of the envelope and all the words are laid out in front of the children. They point to the words and say them, e.g. *cat, pen, hat, box, ten, fox.*

8 Stick the picture of the cat next to the word on the board using sticky tack. Children match their picture cards to the words in front of them.

9 Check answers as a class by sticking your picture cards next to the words on the board.

Extension idea

If you don't want your class to have to deal with so many pieces of paper, leave the word endings and pictures together and only cut out the initial letter sound cards. Children match and glue the letter sounds to complete the words.

Note

If you want to use these cards over and over again, make sets, laminate them and keep them in separate plastic envelopes. Repeat the activity over several classes (for example, during your 'Let's read' slot) until children are able to read the words and match them to the pictures themselves.

c | at

b | ox

f | ox

h | at

p | en

t | en

8.8 Our first words bingo

Outline	Children play phonics bingo (after learning letter-sound relationships).
Focus	*bus, cat, dog, fan, hat, leg, net, pig, sun, ten*
Age	4–6
Time	10–15 minutes
Materials	A bingo card for each child, one set of picture cards, an envelope, small squares of card (six per child).
Preparation	Photocopy and cut out enough bingo cards (see pages 211–212 or the website) so there is one for each child. Photocopy and cut up one set of picture cards (page 213) and put them in an envelope. Cut up six pieces of card for each child (to cover the words on the bingo card).

Procedure

1   Give a bingo card and six pieces of card or paper to each child or pair of children.
2   Hold up the envelope containing the picture cards. Take one picture out of the envelope and show it to the class. Say, e.g. *The word is… h-a-t. hat! Have you got 'hat'?* The children look at the words on their bingo card to see if they have the same one. If they have, they cover it with a square of card or paper. Go around and help. Say, e.g. *That's right, Miren, you've got 'hat'. Put a square on hat.* Then take another picture out of the envelope (e.g. *The next word's sun – s-u-n! Have you got 'sun'? Put a square on 'sun', Marcos.*)
3   Continue in this way. The first child / pair to cover all the words on their card is the winner (if you have more than six children there will be more than one winner). You could give out stickers as prizes.

Variation

Once the children are familiar with the game, they take turns to come and take the next picture card from the envelope. Say, e.g. *It's your turn. Pull out a picture. What is it? Bus! B–u–s.*

Extension ideas

• Play a matching game using the same set of words and pictures ('pelmanism'). Photocopy a set of word cards on coloured card and a set of pictures on another colour card. Cut up the sets and put them in envelopes. In groups of three or four, children place the cards face down on the table. They take turns trying to match a word and picture card. When a child matches two cards correctly, they keep them. The winner is the player with the most pairs at the end of the game. Encourage children to say the words as they turn the cards over, whether they make a match or not.

• Keep sets of word cards and pictures to use at the beginning of class or for early finishers. In pairs, children match the words to the pictures.

Note

Once the children have learned the 26 letter sounds and have started to blend sounds, they will be able to read some other short words, e.g. *ant, bag, bat, bed, big, box, dad, egg, fox, fun, gum, hop, hot, in, on, jam, jet, jug, lip, mat, man, mum, mop, mix, nut, off, pan, peg, pen, pot, red, run, sit, six, top, up, van, yes, zip.* With help, older children can learn to read words starting with initial and final blends, such as: *clap, drum, frog, hand, help, jump, nest, step, stop, tent, wind.*

bin	cat	fan
leg	sun	ten

bus	dog	hat
net	sun	ten

bin	dog	fan
net	leg	sun

bus	cat	hat
dog	leg	bin

bin	fan	hat
sun	bus	net

bus	fan	dog
leg	sun	ten

From *Activities for Very Young Learners* © Cambridge University Press 2017

8.9 Early writing: back drawing and other ideas

Outline	Children play a game to practise forming and saying the letter sounds or numbers.
Focus	Letters of the alphabet, letter-sound correspondences, numbers 1–10
Age	4–6
Time	5–10 minutes
Materials	A whiteboard and marker or letter sound flashcards.
Preparation	None

Procedure

1 Demonstrate the activity by asking two children to come to the front. The children stand back to back. Tell one child that they are going to write. The other child closes their eyes.

2 Say *Don't say the letter sound*. Write a letter on the board, e.g. *n* and show the letter card to the child who is going to write. The child 'writes' the letter on the other child's back. The child who has their eyes closed guesses the letter by saying the letter sound (e.g. *nnnnn*). Ask the class to confirm the answer.

3 Children sit in two rows, facing in the same direction.

4 Get the children who are sitting in the second row to hold up their writing finger. Tell the children in the first row to close their eyes.

5 On the board, draw a letter for the children who are writing to copy. Say *Shhh! Don't say, draw!*

6 Children draw the letter on their partner's back. The children in the front row guess by making the sound. Ask *Is that right? What letter sound is it?* Confirm by saying, e.g. *Yes, it's b! Say b – b – b, everyone*. The whole class says the sound.

7 When all or most of the children have guessed the letter sound, draw another letter on the board.

8 After you've done four or five letters, ask the children to swap places, so that those who were drawing now have their eyes closed. Repeat the game with different letters.

Variation

Use this activity to practise writing numbers. Write numbers 1–10 on the board instead of letters, as children write on each other's backs. This is a fun, no-preparation activity, suitable for a Warmer at the start of the lesson.

Extension ideas

• Write the letters in the air. Stand with your back to the children and draw the letter shapes (using your magic wand, if you like). The children copy your movements.

• The children can practise writing letters in sand or shaving foam. You will need some plastic trays or paper plates. Sprinkle sand or spray foam on each tray / plate. Say the letter sound correspondences. Children take turns writing the letter in the sand or foam with their fingers. Hold up letter cards or write the letters on the board so they can check.

• Children make the letters out of plasticine as you say the letter sounds.

• Use mini-whiteboards. Say letter sounds for older children to practise writing.

8.10 The shopping list game

Outline	Children play a dice game to encourage them to read words where the letter-sound correspondences are not so clear.
Focus	Numbers 1–6, *apples, bananas, carrots, eggs, milk, pizza; What number is it? It's (three). Whose turn is it? It's my / your turn.*
Age	4–7
Time	15–20 minutes
Materials	Dice (preferably large soft ones) and a plastic container for each group, scissors, glue and crayons, a copy of the *Shopping list* worksheet (see page 217) for each child, sticky tack.
Preparation	Arrange the tables so that children can play the game in groups of three or four. On each table you need a dice, scissors, glue and a box of crayons. Photocopy the *Shopping list* handout (one per child) on page 217 (or see the website).
	Cut up your set of food pictures (with the food coloured in) so you can demonstrate the game.

Procedure

1   Demonstrate the game before giving out photocopies or materials. On the whiteboard, draw a large shopping basket like the one on the *Shopping list* worksheet. In a column next to it, write the numbers 1 to 6. Next to each number write a food item, as follows: *1 apples; 2 bananas; 3 carrots; 4 eggs; 5 milk; 6 pizza.* Draw a box next to each word on your list. If your cut-out food items are big enough for the class to see, stick them next to each numbered word. As you stick (or draw) each food item, ask *What are they / is it? That's right, they're apples / it's a pizza!*

2   Stick your six food cards on the board using sticky tack. Roll a large dice on the floor. Ask *What number is it? Yes, it's a …* Point to the same number on the key on the board, e.g. 6 and say *Number 6 is pizza.* Take the pizza card and stick it in the shopping basket on the board. Say *Look! Pizza is number six. I'm putting the pizza in my basket.* Tick the box next to the word *pizza* on the board.

3   Roll the dice again. Say, e.g. *Look! It's a one. Now I'm putting the apples in my basket.* Tick the box next to *apples* on the board.

4   Tell children that they can only roll the dice once on their turn and then they have to pass it on. If they roll a number they already have the picture for, they miss a turn. You could also add a rule that the dice must stay on the table when the child rolls it or they miss a turn.

5   Give out the *Shopping list* worksheets and scissors. Children cut the paper in half, and write their name on the half with the shopping basket. They cut the top half of the handout into six cards, separating the food from the shopping list. Collect the scissors before starting the game.

6   Children play the game in groups, taking turns to roll the dice to complete their shopping by ticking the boxes on the shopping lists and putting the food cards on their baskets. Encourage them to say the numbers and the food they collect in English. Ask *Whose turn it is?* and teach *It's my / your turn.* Let children keep playing until all the baskets are full and the shopping lists completed.

Variation

Children stick the food to their baskets and colour their pictures. Display the finished pictures.

Extension ideas

- Adapt the game to practise different vocabulary sets, for example, draw a square for a toy box and a key with toys (*1 – car, 2 – doll, 3 – ball, 4 – kite, 5 teddy, 6 robot*).
- Play this as a team game, by drawing two shopping baskets on the whiteboard. Photocopy the food cards and shopping list twice, enlarging by 200% and cutting them out. Give each team a shopping list and a pencil. Stick one set of cards on each side of the board, in a column with the corresponding numbers. Teams take turns throwing the dice and sticking their shopping in the baskets. The first team to complete their shopping is the winner.

 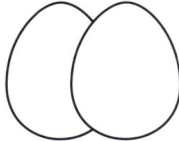

Shopping list _____

1. apples _____

2. bananas _____

3. carrots _____

4. eggs _____

5. milk _____

6. pizza _____

Name.......................................

8.11 Our class book

Outline	Children draw pictures to illustrate a sentence about themselves. The pictures and captions are put together to make a book.
Focus	Talking about likes, e.g. *Alba likes tigers. June likes pink flowers. Unax likes chocolate cake. Jon likes football. Hector likes his robot.* Revision of vocabulary sets, e.g. colours, animals, objects, food, toys, sports and hobbies.
Age	5–7
Time	10–20 minutes over two or three lessons
Materials	A piece of paper for each child, crayons, a black marker pen, a stapler.
Preparation	Staple some pages together to show the children how to make their book.

Procedure

1 Write your name on the board (e.g. *Terry*). Say *I like…* and draw a picture of something you like, for example, a cat (it needs to be a word your class know). Write *Terry likes cats.* on the board.

2 Ask a confident child to come to the board. Write their name and *likes*. Ask questions with *Do you like …?* until the child says *Yes*, for example, *Do you like flowers? Do you like tennis? Do you like pizza?* Complete the sentence on the board, e.g. *Jessica likes tennis.*

3 Give each child a piece of paper and crayons. They draw a picture of what they like. Go around the class, asking *What do you like?* Write a sentence under each child's picture, similar to the ones on the board: *(Name) likes …*

4 Early finishers can add more things they like to the picture – you don't have to write everything they draw.

5 Collect all the pages and staple them together to make a class book, if possible adding a page about yourself.

6 'Read' your class book together. Show the pictures and say, e.g. *June likes pink flowers. Unax likes chocolate cake… look! What else does he like? Yes, swimming! And I like English! Look – I'm saying 'Hello' to my class.* If you return to the book regularly, you will find that the children begin to join in with the sentences.

Extension ideas

• Use cardboard to make front and back covers for your class book. If you have permission from the children's parents, take a photo of the whole class to use as the cover picture.

• At the end of the year, take the pages of the book apart so that children can take their page(s) home.

8.12 Letter writing

Outline	The children receive a letter and send a reply as a class.
Focus	*letter, Dear, Love*, revision of vocabulary
Age	5–7
Time	15–20 minutes
Materials	A letter, addressed to your class, in an envelope with a stamp on it, a piece of paper and pen (or two postcards).
	Optional: A photo of the letter writer (e.g. your class mascot) on holiday.
Preparation	Decide who could go 'on holiday' from your school. It must be someone that your children know (for example, the robot that lives in the toy box, your class puppet or teddy bear or a real person, such as the headteacher). Make sure this toy / person is not in class on the day your children 'receive' the letter.
	Write a letter as if it were from the toy / person (see Step 2 below) and put it in an envelope. Seal the envelope. If possible, prepare a photo of the toy / person on holiday (e.g. in a forest, in a hotel room, on the beach).

Procedure

1 Show the letter the children have 'received'. Read the address (your class) and open the letter, with great excitement. If you have a photograph of the writer on holiday, hold it up and ask *Who's this?*

2 Open the letter and read it. See the example below, but note that your letter needs to feature the toy / person you have chosen and your country. It can also cover topics you are working on in class.

> Dear class,
>
> How are you? I'm happy! I'm in England. It's very cold here. What's the weather like in Spain? What are you doing today in class? Please write to me. I miss you!
>
> Love,
> Rita Robot

3 Write a reply to the letter on the board, starting *Dear ..., Thank you for your letter ...* Elicit ideas of what to write about from the children.

4 Once you have composed the letter on the board, write it again on paper. Here is an example:

> Dear Rita Robot,
>
> Thank you for your letter and the photo. We are fine. It's hot today.
> We sang a song about elephants in class today.
> Please come back soon.
>
> Love,

5 Get all the children to write or trace their names at the bottom of the letter.

6 Put the letter in an envelope, address it and 'send' it to the writer of the first letter. When the toy / person returns to school, they can bring the letter and say *Thank you for your letter. I loved it!*

Extension ideas

- If a visitor comes to class (a teacher, storyteller or someone to talk about their job, for example), write a 'thank you' letter together, saying what the children learned from the visitor or liked most about the visit.
- If you talk about a relative or a friend and have shown the children photos of this person, you could ask them to write a letter to your class. Writing a reply would be a very authentic experience and receiving a letter from your class would no doubt delight your relative or friend, too.

Index

Note: Activity titles are shown in **bold** and locators for figures are shown in *italics*.